Bloom's Modern Critical Views

Bloom's Modern Critical Views

HENRIK IBSEN
New Edition

Edited and with an introduction by
Harold Bloom
Sterling Professor of the Humanities
Yale University

BLOOM'S
LITERARY CRITICISM
An Infobase Learning Company

Bloom's Modern Critical Views: Henrik Ibsen—New Edition
Copyright © 2011 by Infobase Learning
Introduction © 2011 by Harold Bloom

Bloom's Literary Criticism
An imprint of Infobase Learning
132 West 31st Street
New York NY 10001

Library of Congress Cataloging-in-Publication Data
Henrik Ibsen / edited and with an introduction by Harold Bloom. — New ed.
    p. cm. — (Bloom's modern critical views)
Includes bibliographical references and index.
ISBN 978-1-60413-577-0 (hardcover)
1. Ibsen, Henrik, 1828–1906—Criticism and interpretation.   I. Bloom, Harold.
PT8895.H432 2011
839.8'226—dc22

                        2010044810

Bloom's Literary Criticism books are available at special discounts when purchased in bulk quantities for businesses, associations, institutions, or sales promotions. Please call our Special Sales Department in New York at (212) 967-8800 or (800) 322-8755.

You can find Bloom's Literary Criticism on the World Wide Web at
http://www.chelseahouse.com

Contributing editor: Pamela Loos
Cover designed by Takeshi Takahashi
Composition by IBT Global, Troy NY
Cover printed by IBT Global, Troy NY
Book printed and bound by IBT Global, Troy NY
Date printed: March 2011
Printed in the United States of America

10 9 8 7 6 5 4 3 2 1

This book is printed on acid-free paper.

All links and Web addresses were checked and verified to be correct at the time of publication. Because of the dynamic nature of the Web, some addresses and links may have changed since publication and may no longer be valid.

Contents

Editor's Note

My introduction asserts Ibsen's status as a visionary whose best works, including *Brand, Emperor and Galilean,* and *Peer Gynt,* operate on a vast scale. Evert Sprinchorn explores the intersection of Ibsen and the actorly personae who have transformed his characters through the years. Errol Durbach then examines the secular theodicy that informed the dramatist's romantic leanings.

James Walter McFarlane suggests that a trio of Ibsen's dramas were written in response to the drubbing *Ghosts* received at the hands of Norwegian critics and theatergoers. Inga-Stina Ewbank then posits the two works Ibsen set in Rome, *Catiline* and *Emperor and Galilean,* as touchstones for the transmission of Shakespearean influence.

Eric Bentley returns to the notion of reading versus performance and its influence on Ibsen's critical legacy, followed by Tanya Thresher's assessment of the effect language and power have on the women of *Hedda Gabler.*

Kristin Brunnemer takes up the feminist legacy of *A Doll's House.* Terrance McConnell concludes the volume by retreading the moral battleground that anchors *An Enemy of the People.*

Introduction

$\mathbf{M}$y favorite plays by Ibsen would include *Brand* and the epic *Emperor and Galilean*, as well as *Peer Gynt* and *Hedda Gabler.* Though previously I had been baffled by Brian Johnston's (*The Ibsen Cycle*) insistence on the close parallel between Hegel's *Phenomenology of Mind* and Ibsen's final twelve plays, Johnston indeed does demonstrate that Ibsen's work fits very well into the Hegelian vision of tragedy. Whether or not this resulted from the direct influences upon Ibsen, like Shakespeare and Hegel, Ibsen is a world visionary who works on a vast scale. Parallels between the three necessarily abound.

Brand and the Emperor Julian are Ibsen's most heroic characters, yet they are hero-villains in the Shakespearean mode. This doubleness applies still more strongly to Hedda Gabler and to later figures like Solness and Rubek. For Thomas Van Laan, Hedda Gabler is a version of Shakespeare's Cleopatra; I would add Iago to the mix. The Ibsenite hero-villains, like the Shakespearean, are trollish or daemonic; the great exception is Peer Gynt, whose comic genius (like Falstaff's), redeems him from most taints of trollishness. The Emperor Julian has his Macbeth aspect, but Peer is a natural man and amiable scamp who may behave like a hero-villain but who charms himself, his fellow characters, and the audience into forgiving everything. Call Peer Gynt, like Ibsen himself, a borderline troll, but far gentler than his fiercer creator. For Ibsen's true self-portrait, we can turn to Hedda Gabler, a worthy rival of Shakespeare's Cleopatra.

*   *   *

Ibsen's vast range is allied to his uncanny ability to transcend genre; in both respects he is like Shakespeare, the dominant though frequently hidden

1

influence upon his work. Shakespeare wrote his 38 (or so) plays in a quarter century; Ibsen composed for 50 years, and gave us 25 plays. His masterpieces, in my judgment, include *Brand*, *Peer Gynt*, *Emperor and Galilean*, in the period 1865–73, with *Hedda Gabler* as a great postlude in 1890. *Peer Gynt* and *Hedda Gabler* retain their popularity but do not seem so frequently performed as what are taken to be Ibsen's "social dramas": *A Doll's House*, *Ghosts*, *An Enemy of the People*, *The Wild Duck*, and the earlier *Pillars of Society*. His final period, after he turned 60, gave us four great visionary plays: *The Lady from the Sea*, *The Master Builder*, *John Gabriel Borkman*, and *When We Dead Awaken*. Yet all of Ibsen is visionary drama; he inherited Shakespeare's invention of the human, characters capable of overhearing themselves, and his mastery of inwardness is second only to Shakespeare's. I will confine myself, in this introduction, to brief accounts of only two plays: *Brand* and *Hedda Gabler*, or rather to the two sublime characters who give their names to these dramas.

Ibsen, who could be caustic, had a powerful aversion to Strindberg. "I have always liked storms," he wrote in a letter to his sister, a fondness that helps explain his purchase of a large portrait of Strindberg, which he hung on the wall of his study. Under the baleful gaze of his enemy, whom he considered "delightfully mad," Ibsen was spurred on to even more exuberance in his final plays, *John Gabriel Borkman* and the apocalyptic *When We Dead Awaken*. Earlier, in response to *Hedda Gabler*, where he found himself portrayed as Lovberg, the poet inspired to suicide by the demonic Hedda, Strindberg expressed his own fury:

> It seems to me that Ibsen realizes that I shall inherit the crown when he is finished. He hates me mentally. . . . And now the decrepit old troll seems to hand me the revolver! . . . I shall survive him and many others, and the day *The Father* kills *Hedda Gabler*, I shall stick the gun in the old troll's neck.

The wild Strindberg was more overtly trollish than the socially conforming Ibsen, but Strindberg accurately diagnosed his unwelcome precursor as an "old troll." Trolls are not easy to define, particularly when they are thoroughly mixed into the human. If you think of the later Freudian myth of the rival drives of love and death, Eros and Thanatos, you get close to human trollishness. Ibsen's trollish figures are both doom eager and desperate for more life; they are Ibsen's Shakespearean energies personified. Thomas Van Laan traces Hedda Gabler's debt to Shakespeare's Cleopatra, and on the level of deliberate allusion, that is definitely correct. But the deeper, more implicit model for Hedda is "honest Iago," the most trollish of all Shakespearean characters. Ibsen once told an interviewer that: "There must be troll in what I write," and one can wonder if he ever fully enjoyed the apparent Shakespearean detachment that he cultivated. No one should miss either the troll in Ibsen himself or the presence of Ibsen in Brand, Hedda Gabler, Peer Gynt, and all their fellow protagonists. Perhaps Falstaff and Hamlet each had a link to Shakespeare's own personality and character, but such a surmise can only be imaginative. Ibsen is not Shakespeare; the dramatist of the great trolls was as late romantic as they were: vitalistic, close to nihilistic, determined to turn life into the true work of art.

Brand speaks of "the poem of my life"; if he is a man of God, that god seems more Dionysus than Yahweh. Guilt, to a Dionysiac hero, has nothing to do with Original Sin, but rather reflects a failure to sustain ecstasy. Compromising in any way, with anything or anyone, is totally alien to Brand. He seeks only the Sublime, which he calls God, yet other names (including Brand's own) seem more accurate. Destroying the lives of those one loves best is hardly a path to God. Brand's capacity for suffering seems infinite, but why need he immerse those who care most for him in suffering that they cannot sustain? Ibsen is aware that *Brand* is not a "religious drama"; Brand, according to the dramatist, could also have been a sculptor or politician. W.H. Auden strongly disagreed. Himself a Kierkegaardian, Auden regarded Brand as an apostle, someone who knows only "that he is called upon to forsake everything he has been, to venture into an unknown and probably unpleasant future." One can wonder if Auden was correct in so assimilating Brand to Kierkegaard's difficult question of "becoming a Christian" in a country ostensibly already Christian. Auden himself points to the clear Nietzschean elements in Brand's exaltation of the will. If Brand is an apostle, then the message he carries was given to him by the god Dionysus, who in one of his aspects is something of a troll.

Brand fascinates, though he also alienates himself from us. Even as he beholds the avalanche coming down upon him, he cries out to God: "Answer!" We shudder at the sublimity of the Brandian will, and yet we are not allowed to sympathize with Brand. Hedda Gabler, even more fascinating, powerfully provokes something of the same dramatic sympathy that Iago inspires in us. Hedda is the greatest figure in all Ibsen, possibly because she is Ibsen. "Men and women don't belong in the same century," the playwright enigmatically remarked. I think Ibsen would have said the same of the twentieth century, or the twenty-first, or any whatsoever.

As a demon or half-troll, Hedda emulates Iago by writing a tragic farce in which she and the other protagonists are caught in the net of her devisings. Oscar Wilde, accurate always, said he "felt pity and terror, as though the play had been Greek." Just as deftly, Wilde could have added: "or *Othello*." Hedda, who fears boring herself to death, finds Iago's cure for ennui: Murder (or ruin) your fellow characters. Ibsen's marvelous woman shoots herself in the fore-head, in the mode of Iago affirming: "from this time forth I never shall speak word," as he prepares to die silently under torture. Both Hedda and Iago are sublime solipsists, dramatists of the self at the expense of all others. And both are too grand for our mere disapproval. They stimulate our fear and our pity, as do Brand and Solness and so many of Ibsen's titans. The exception is Peer Gynt, who escapes into comedy.

EVERT SPRINCHORN

Ibsen and the Actors

One of the peculiarities of the art of the theatre is that the difference between the score and the performance tends to be greater than in the other performing arts. The reason for this is that the actor is not an instrument, at least not in the sense that an oboe is. An oboe remains an oboe whatever piece is being played, but Burbage was not Betterton, Betterton was not Booth, Booth was not Barrymore, although they all played Hamlet. An oboe exists apart from the score, but Hamlet does not. The notes that an oboist plays do not give shape to an oboe, while Hamlet can be defined only by what he says and does in the script. If a dramatic part is a complicated one, it will be virtually impossible for an actor to play all the notes that make up the character. As Hamlet says, 'You would play upon me; you would seem to know my stops; you would pluck out the heart of my mystery. . . . Do you think I am easier to be played on than a pipe? Call me what instrument you will, though you can fret me, yet you cannot play upon me.' If, on the other hand, the character in the script is rather simple, a strong actor can enhance the part and add to the mystery. Hamlet remains Hamlet in spite of the number of actors who have played him, but Mathias in *The Bells* is to those who know him at all the Mathias that Henry Irving created.

The personality of an actor can brighten a dull script and transform the improbabilities of an idiotic plot into the certainties of his stage presence.

From *Ibsen and the Theatre: The Dramatist in Production*, edited by Errol Durbach, pp. 118–30. Copyright © 1980 by Errol Durbach.

All too often, however, a great actor adulterates a rich and profound script by making it serve merely as a display case for his personality. Anyone interested in great acting is not likely to object strenuously to this, since great acting is as rare as great playwriting, though literary scholars are sure to be offended. But everyone is offended when an ordinary actor turns a rich and complicated part into a theatrical stereotype. The history of acting affords a number of examples of this sort of artistic debasement.

In Sheridan's play *The School for Scandal*, Sir Peter Teazle, a man of fifty years or more, is married to an attractive girl half his age. He and she are constantly quarrelling with each other, but their quarrels are only lovers' tiffs. Sir Peter himself says, 'I think she never appears to such advantage as when she is doing everything in her power to plague me.' Sheridan sees to it that the couple stays married at the end of the play, and indicates that the flirtatious Lady Teazle will settle down to a happy life with Sir Peter. When the role was originally acted, Sir Peter was represented as a vigorous man, stimulated by his wife's vivacity and high spirits. But the succeeding generations of actors portrayed Sir Peter as a decrepit old man. They turned him into a laughing-stock who deserved to be ridiculed for having supposed that December could mate with May. Why the change? Because it was easier for mediocre actors to raise a laugh by acting the wheezing, shuffling, old man than to get a lasting smile by acting the middle-aged man who admires his wife's spirit and ebullience and is vigorous, charming, and solicitous enough to be loved by her.

It might be thought that dramatic characters when recreated by succeeding generations of actors would grow richer and more complicated, with subtle traits and telling acting points being invented by imaginative actors and passed on to others. But such is often not the case. One reason for this is that dramatic characters are rooted in their time, and when transported to another time they lose their fragrance and bouquet. Another reason is that great acting parts, with the enormous demands that they make, are constantly being reduced to the actor's and director's level of ability, intelligence, and knowledge. All too often actors do not do their homework properly. They settle for a characterisation that fits one of the stereotypes they are familiar with. They make Sir Peter into a silly old man because silly old men are (or were) laughable and easy to play. Such actors may make the unskilful laugh, but they cannot but make the judicious grieve.

Both these reasons help account for the prevailing lacklustre way of acting Ibsen, especially in America. There is yet another reason, however, which applies especially to Ibsen. This has to do with the stereotype to which we have reduced Ibsen. Although we hear much about his power of characterisation, the fact is that he is usually played for his ideas. We go to see an Ibsen play because for once we want an intellectual evening in the theatre or because we wish to pay tribute to a man who helped us think the right things. Though actors and actresses may regard the big Ibsen parts as living characters, they are played as if they incarnated certain social or philosophical ideas. Nora and Hedda, for example, are nowadays usually represented essentially as women trapped in a man's world, while the other characters around them exist primarily to point up the theme or dominant idea.

This approach is certainly not wrong in itself, but to stress it, as nearly everyone does, is to distort the characters and warp the real drama of the plays. To portray Nora simply as a woman who has not been able to be herself because men have always told her what to be is to ignore what it is in her that makes her realise this when thousands of other women in the same situation never came to any such realisation. Making her purely a feminist ahead of her time is like making Sir Peter merely an old man ahead of his time.

Nora has managed to stand up to this reductionist approach fairly well, but the effect on her husband Torvald Helmer has been disastrous. He has become a caricature, a cardboard husband who has no business on the stage with Nora. The people who stage *A Doll's House* obviously consider him a secondary figure, a sparring partner for Nora. It is never a real match that we see, only a demonstration of Nora's prowess as a fighter for women's rights. Within the past few years Nora has been acted by Jane Fonda, Claire Bloom, and Liv Ullmann, and everyone knows who they are. But who played Torvald opposite them? *A Doll's House* has degenerated into a vehicle for a star. Yet, ironically and fittingly, the star has not gained by this; she has lost.

For *A Doll's House* was not written as a vehicle for the actress. When it was to be staged for the first time in Stockholm, Ibsen let it be known that he wanted Gustaf Fredrikson to play the part of Torvald. Now Fredrikson was to the Stockholm stage of the 1870s what Cary Grant was to the Hollywood film of the 1930s and 1940s. Fredrikson was a matinee idol before there was such a thing, the popular star of drawing-room comedy and light melodrama, admired for his elegance and charm, and these were the qualities that Ibsen believed essential to the characterisation of Torvald.[1] The Torvalds I have seen were as charming and elegant as Punch in a puppet show. Imagine how our attitude toward the play would change if we saw the latest movie idol (assuming he had some genuine talent) as Torvald opposite a strong but not more commanding actress. Not a word of dialogue would have to be changed in order for everything to change. It would be an entirely different play.

The idea may seem unsound and impractical. Why has there not been a recent production of *A Doll's House* with a captivating Torvald? Why did not some American matinee idol play the part? Why did not Alfred Lunt play Torvald to Lynn Fontanne's Nora? Or Laurence Olivier to Vivien Leigh's Nora? Or even consider it? The reason of course is that Torvald is considered to be a thankless role. Ibsen has depicted him as a self-centred, rather insensitive man, who, when the threat of blackmail has been removed, exclaims not, '*We* are saved, Nora!' but, '*I* am saved!' If Ibsen wanted him to be charming and ingratiating, why did he make him so unsympathetic in our eyes? Again we know the reason. Ibsen was writing at a time when the sympathies of the audience would lie mainly with the husband, with Torvald, whatever sort of man he was. To give Nora a fighting chance in the struggle for the sympathies of the audience Ibsen had to darken the character of Torvald. It was in the final draft of the play that Ibsen changed '*We* are saved!' to '*I* am saved!' In the first German production of the play Nora did not leave her husband: the actress playing the part refused to represent such an immoral, unmotherly, and unnatural act on the stage. But just as Ibsen in 1879 had to give Torvald extra weight to carry in order to give Nora a fighting chance, so nowadays we must re-examine the handicaps if we wish not only to hear the words Ibsen gave his actors to speak but also to feel the tension behind them.

Once Nora and Torvald are allowed to exist as characters rather than as pieces in the campaign for the liberation of women, they become vivid and disturbingly real, and much more challenging to actors than the Nora and Torvald one ordinarily sees on stage. Torvald is after all a good father to his three children, and the attentive and ardent lover of his wife. An ambitious man with a promising career ahead of him, he is a conscientious provider who worked so hard for his family that his health collapsed. He has given Nora all the material things and all the sexual attention that any young wife could reasonably desire. He loves beautiful things, and not least his pretty wife. In fact his sense of beauty is more highly developed than hers. He plays the piano; he choreographs Nora's dance; and he does not like to see women knitting because the arm movements are ugly. And since he is fundamentally an aesthete he tends to treat Nora as a pretty object.

For years Nora appreciated all that Torvald did for her and the children as much as a normal wife would. But the change in their relationship comes about because Nora is not a normal woman. She is compulsive, highly imaginative, and very much inclined to go to extremes. She is more than a put-upon creature who resolves to fight on the barricades for the feminist cause. And Torvald is more than a selfish husband who looks upon his wife as part of his chattels personal. Like Nora, he has been formed or conditioned by social conventions and attitudes and made to play a part that by nature he is perhaps not well suited for. Bernard Shaw said that his *Candida* was a 'counterblast to Ibsen's *A Doll's House*, showing that in the real typical doll's house it is the man who is the doll.'[2] The truth is that the last part of Ibsen's play is the Shavian counterblast to the first part, for Torvald turns out to have been the doll all along. Torvald has regarded himself as the breadwinner in the family, the main support of his wife and children, as any decent husband would like to regard himself. When he discovers that it was Nora who sustained the family during the crucial months of his illness, it is no wonder that he is profoundly shaken. His whole concept of himself has been shattered—a concept imposed on him by society. He has unknowingly been the wife in the family. Therein lies a dramatic self-recognition that passes virtually unnoticed because all eyes are on Nora.

When Nora leaves him, she says that they might live together in a true marriage only if a great miracle occurred, a miracle of miracles. She can only mean a miracle by which Torvald would become more a wife and she more a husband. Ibsen appears to be hinting at unisexual marriage, and Torvald in the last moment of the play is willing to consider the possibility. But the change that is taking place in the apparently rigid and unyielding Torvald is never brought out in production. Only Nora is allowed to be transformed. Torvald must remain a stick-in-the-mud. This brings us back to the question of Nora's character. Who is the real Nora—the flighty, macaroon-eating girl of the first act or the mission-minded woman of the last? There was a time when critics concerned themselves about the transformation of Nora and wondered whether her emergence as an independent spirit in the last part of the play was credible. By now, however, most actresses who undertake the role know that the strong-willed Nora is present even in the opening scenes. Only there she is playing a game, a game that has become practically second nature to her, pretending to be her husband's plaything yet knowing that he owes his very life to her. The actress must play both aspects of Nora, a task that is not difficult since Ibsen presents a Nora who at the rise of the curtain has almost made up her mind to assert her right to individuality.[3]

However, there is another aspect to the character that invariably fails to manifest itself in production because Nora is always thought of as a kind of saint, a martyr to the feminist cause, without any thought being given to what it is that makes a saint. To understand Nora fully the actress must not concern herself with the question: how could the giddy woman of the first part become the strong woman of the last act? She must ask what kind of woman is this Nora who is willing to leave her husband and children, not for another man, mind you, but in order to find out how much validity there is in the ideas that have been inculcated in her since she was a child. There were any number of women in Ibsen's time who had greater cause to rebel, women with cruel and abusive husbands; women without any children to bind them to home and husband, women without the comforts of a middle-class house. What is there in Nora, a woman who has all a woman of her time—and perhaps of our time—could reasonably hope for, that makes her see the injustice of a world that everyone else accepts, and rebel against it? What is it that sets her apart from all the other women who meekly accepted their lot even when their lot was much worse than Nora's?[4]

It is obvious that Ibsen has carefully and deliberately seen to it that Nora does not have the ordinary reasons for leaving her husband. Apparently she leaves Torvald because he does not live up to her ideal. All along she has imagined that Torvald is a kind of romantic hero, as willing to make sacrifices as she is. When, instead of offering to sacrifice his name and reputation for her sake, he upbraids her as an unprincipled woman, she realises she has been living with a man she does not really know. The man she thought she had married was the product of her romantic imagination. As a man of his times Torvald is partly responsible for fostering these romantic notions about male and female roles, notions that are as flattering to him as they are impossible for him to live up to.

Let me indicate very quickly what Ibsen lets us learn about Nora. She has been dominated by men all her life, her mother having died when Nora was very young. As a child she was completely under the spell of her father, and as a wife she has been completely under the spell of her husband. She has always been protected, cared for, and perhaps spoiled. This has made her egocentric, and indifferent to the sufferings of others. She knew of the plight of her good friend Christine but never bothered to communicate with her. She flirts cruelly with Dr Rank and toys with his deep affection for her, drawing him on to find out how strong her hold over him actually is. Most revealing of all is the way she went about saving her husband. She was not compelled to borrow from a stranger and forge her father's signature on a promissory note. She could have turned to friends of her husband for the necessary money; any other woman would have done so. But Nora knew that if she turned to one of Torvald's friends for help, she would have had to share her role of saviour with someone else. By borrowing from a stranger and forging her father's signature, she sees herself as sparing the sufferings of two people, her husband who is ill and her father who is dying. Thus the doll becomes the rescuer of the men who made her a doll. She revels in the role of saviour, proving herself ultimately superior to her husband, secretly enjoying the reversal of roles, and knowing that from now on Torvald will always and inescapably be in her debt. In her imagination she foresees the time when, growing old and less attractive to Torvald, she can reveal how she saved him. It is her insurance policy against the future. The 'most wonderful thing of all' of which she speaks is the gratitude toward her that Torvald must feel when he eventually learns the truth. That moment is suddenly brought from the distant future into the present when Krogstad, from whom she borrowed the money, threatens to expose her as a criminal. Responding hysterically to this threat, she lets her thoughts rush ahead. If she viewed her situation calmly, she would realise that no serious crime had been committed; the only threat is to Torvald's reputation. Now she imagines Torvald interceding on her behalf, taking her crime on his shoulders, behaving as the men in her life have always done, protecting her, and thereby being superior to her. But this time it will be different. She will forestall Torvald, deny his guilt to the world, and then drown herself. Dying for Torvald's sake, she will forever remain superior to him.

In this brilliant analysis, which I have extracted from a probing commentary written by a psychiatrist in 1907, we have the real Nora.[5] Here we see what makes the martyr and feminist who slams he door on husband and children. The actress who endeavours to portray Nora in all her complexity must centre her efforts not on the last scene, the remarkable discussion between the self-righteous husband and the disillusioned wife, a scene that plays itself, but on the tarantella scene that Ibsen intended as the climax of the drama and that brings the curtain down on the second act. In her Italian costume, which is associated with the journey to the south that saved her husband's life, Nora is still the plaything of her husband. But the frenetic dance that she performs and that Torvald feels compelled to interrupt is in her mind a sacrificial dance. In thirty-one hours she will throw herself into the river for her husband's sake. The dancing doll will become the human martyr, and this time not in secret. In that hysterical tarantella the two sides of Nora reveal themselves simultaneously. (The symbolism of the dance is equally appropriate whether the tarantella is thought of as the dance caused by the bite of the tarantula or as the dance meant to drive the spider's poison from the victim's system.)

The reverse side of the noble feminist is what one does not see on stage. But any actress who wants to represent the woman Ibsen created must act the double intention, must act both Noras, the Nora who is deceitful yet honest, theatrical yet sincere, insensitive and inconsiderate yet willing to give her life for her husband, a woman who is cunning enough to know that she is only playing a game for his benefit, only pretending to be a doll, yet who keeps in her mind a naive, romantic view of him as hero, a woman who sees herself as so much in debt to the male sex that the only possible way she can repay the debt is to give her own life, a woman whose whole world crumbles into dust when she discovers that the one thing she thought was real in it, her husband, proves to be a doll also. What we do see on stage is only, at best, half of this Nora, half of the richest, most complex female character that any dramatist had created since Shakespeare's time.

It has often been said that Chekhov's characters are as complicated as living people, and his plays are frequently compared to icebergs. The script, the printed text, is only the tip of the iceberg. In order to portray a Chekhov character the actor must create from the one-tenth of the character that is plainly visible the nine-tenths that lie submerged. So acting students write imaginary biographies of these characters, improvise new scenes for them, and invent all sorts of business to give the fullest sense of reality to Chekhov's people. Every effort is made to endow these fictional figures with flesh and blood, to dissociate them from abstract ideas, to see to it that they do not become caricatures. In contrast, every effort is made, often unconsciously, to shape Ibsen's creations as the embodiments of ideas. The result has been harmful to both dramatists. Chekhov's characters have been made more complicated than they really are, and Ibsen's less so. Chekhov concerned himself mostly with simple, ordinary people, whose aspirations are relatively modest, and who are not divided against themselves. 'Let us be just as simple and complex as life itself is', said Chekhov. 'People sit down to dine and their happiness is made or destroyed.' His characters are what they seem to be. In portraying them on stage the actor looks for the 'spine' of the character and fleshes it out with true-to-life touches. Of Madame Ranevskaya, one of the choicest roles in the Chekhov canon, Chekhov himself said, 'It is not difficult to play [her]; only one has to find the right key from the very beginning; one has to find a smile and a way of laughing; one must be able to dress.'[6] The major characters in Ibsen—Nora, Hedda, Mrs Alving, Torvald, Gregers, Solness, Allmers—cannot be represented in this simple, direct way, though that is the way they are usually represented. Chekhov's characters are meant to be ordinary people, not very neurotic, not very disturbed. Madame Ranevskaya, a woman with a past, and with a lover waiting for her in Paris, is not nearly as troubled by her conscience as her counterpart in Ibsen would be. For one sentimental moment she speaks of her sins, but she quickly puts the past out of her mind and journeys back to Paris. It is not a question of Chekhov's having less insight into human nature than Ibsen; it is a question of different kinds of people. Ibsen dealt with extremists, people with divided souls. Chekhov did not, except in the case of Constantine Treplev, the failed writer who commits suicide. He belongs in Ibsen, just as Hjalmar Ekdal, who has no understanding of extremists, would be right at home among Chekhov's characters. Chekhov's view of the world was essentially comic; Ibsen's essentially tragic. Chekhov's people take what the world offers; Ibsen's heroes want more than the world could possibly provide.

Gregers Werle in *The Wild Duck* is a uniquely Ibsenian creation, an idealist tormented by guilt, imposing himself where he is not wanted, and wreaking havoc where he thought he was bringing peace and harmony. Everyone knows that in writing *The Wild Duck* Ibsen was repudiating his former crusading self, and that in Gregers he wished to show the harm caused by a zealot bent on making the world live up to his idea of perfection. Even actors know this, or find it out soon enough, and inevitably they end up portraying a Gregers who fits this preconception of the part. And sure enough, every-thing the actor finds in the script appears to fit this preconception. Gregers is harmful: he blunders into the happy Ekdal home and destroys it. His influ-ence is pernicious: little Hedwig commits suicide because of his mad talk. He is a fool: he idolises Hjalmar Ekdal, though it is obvious to every other adult in the play that he is a self-indulgent, lazy, pampered egotist. And to make certain that the audience recognises Gregers from the first moment as a hostile figure, Ibsen has made him repulsive in appearance, ugly of feature and physically clumsy. The portrait verges on caricature.

But suppose we were to examine Gregers without any preconceptions about Ibsen's ideas. We would see all that I have mentioned, but we would see much else besides. We would see a man who had an unhappy childhood, brought up in a house in which mother and father had nothing in common, who saw hate grow between his parents, saw his mother become a hopeless alcoholic, and, seeing his mother decline, came to hate his father. When he was an adolescent, his closest friend was Hjalmar Ekdal, a cheerful, hand-some young man, coddled by the two aunts who reared him and loved by a father who shared with his boy many of the pleasures of life, taking the boy out hunting with him, for example; and those happy days in the forest are the ones father and son relive in their make-believe forest in the garret. Hjalmar had everything that Gregers dreamed of having. And then, when they were both about twenty years old, there occurred the business scandal that ruined the Ekdal family. His father's part in this affair made Gregers detest him all the more, and because of his own silence when his word might have helped the Ekdals, Gregers has ever since been weighed down with the burden of guilt. In trying to lighten that burden he became a crusader, a fanatic crying out to all and sundry, 'Ye shall know the truth and the truth shall make you free', believing that the cure his damaged soul needed must be good for all souls. Having been silent and untruthful at a crucial moment, he has since resolved to speak the truth, convinced that the momentary pain the truth may cost is as nothing compared to the years of anguish he has suffered for shirk-ing the truth. This is the man who comes to the home of Hjalmar Ekdal and finds a god-given opportunity to redeem his own sin against the Ekdal family by telling Hjalmar, the idol of his youth, the truth about Hjalmar's wife and her involvement with old Werle. Monomaniacal and compulsive about the truth, especially about a truth that will allow him to atone for his silence years ago by exposing his father now as he should have exposed him then, Gregers never stops to consider the alternatives. He judges the situation from his own experience. The other side of the question is like the other side of the moon to him. He has never known the kind of happiness that comes when affection and fellow-feeling palliate the truth and make it bearable. His parents had no love for him. He will never be a husband or a father, and he knows it. He is not only psychically ill; he is also physically ill, suffering from some kind of nervous disease. At the end of the play, seeing that Hedwig has committed suicide, he is seized with convulsions ('*krampaktige rykninger*').

All this may not make Gregers appealing, but it does help us to understand him, and understanding is not too far removed from sympathy. However, there is yet another quality in him that is slighted by the actors. Gregers is always presented as oblivious to the feelings of others. He is as gauche emotionally as he is physically. Yet it is Gregers who of all the people in the drama strikes the deepest chords in the child Hedwig. In the most haunting scene in the play Gregers penetrates Hedwig's secret world, speaks of the 'briny depths of the sea', and forges a bond with her that has the strength of absolute faith. She is decidedly the most sympathetic and endearing person in the play. She senses something in Gregers that the others do not. In order to make the outcome convincing what she senses in him must be sensed by the audience, too. That is why it is incumbent on the actor to elevate Gregers in this scene far beyond the usual conception of him as a crazy, demented fool, which is how Dr Relling sees him, and to make him, at least for the moment, a man of spiritual insight whose concerns are with man's highest endeavours. Dr Relling, who believes in the necessity of the life-lie, the need that people have for illusions about themselves, may understand ordinary mortals, but it is Gregers who understands extraordinary beings.

In the scene with Hedwig, Gregers is not some demon casting an evil spell on the child. The scene is infused with all the pain and anguish that Gregers has experienced in life, all his loneliness, and with all the special kind of understanding that he has gained from the unhappiness that he has known. Unless this positive aspect of Gregers is brought out by the actor, something vital to the play will be lost. The scene with Hedwig constitutes the preparation for Hedwig's drastic act at the end of the play. If Gregers is not made fascinating in the way that prophets are fascinating, the workings of Hedwig's mind will be only half comprehensible. If Gregers is seen by the audience only as Dr Relling sees him, and that is the usual way of looking at him, *The Wild Duck* dwindles into a thesis play, Relling is reduced to being the author's mouthpiece, and Gregers appears as only the husk of a living person.

Because actors and directors have failed to explore the depths of Ibsen's characters, we are seeing only a part of the plays that Ibsen wrote, and perhaps only a part of the plays that our grandparents saw. Though there has been a general improvement in acting, our actors and directors have lost some of the insight and instinctive understanding that an earlier generation may have had, since they were closer in time and spirit to the original figures. To regain that lost ground and advance beyond it, it is necessary to look at these characters freshly and to put into the stage representation of them all the apparent inconsistencies, all the convolutions of thought, all the layers of emotional life that lie in the scripts of the plays. Actors now give us the emerging feminist in Nora and the crazy idealist in Gregers. But how much more interesting these characters would be, and how much more controversial and stimulating the plays would become if the actors presented not only the feminist in Nora but also the hysterical woman who is willing to leave husband and children in order to find out whether she alone or the whole world is right; not only the obsessed truth-seeker in Gregers but also the wretchedly unhappy man who can only give meaning to his own life by vicariously living Hjalmar's. Ideas are an essential element in Ibsen's plays, but ideas are made by people and transmitted by people. 'The actor's business', said Bernard Shaw in reviewing one of Ibsen's plays, 'is not to supply an idea with a sounding board, but with a credible, simple, and natural human being to utter it when its time comes and not before.'[7]

And ultimately people are more complex and controversial than ideas. 'Why is there so much concern about what my plays mean?' asked Ibsen. 'We all act and write under the influence of some idea or other. The question is: have I succeeded in creating a good drama with living persons?'[8] He usually succeeded, but all too often the actors have not.

Notes

1. See Ibsen's letter to the Royal Theatre, Stockholm, 1 October 1879, in *Ibsens brevväxling med Dramatiska teatern*, ed. Stig Torsslow (Stockholm, 1973), p. 22.

2. Letter to Beverley Baxter, in the *Evening Standard*, London, 30 November 1944; reprinted in *A Casebook on Candida*, ed. Stephen S. Stanton (New York, 1962), p. 158.

3. See Henry Rose, *Henrik Ibsen: Poet, Mystic and Moralist* (London, 1913), p. 41.

4. Magdalene Thoresen, the step-mother of Ibsen's wife, regarded Nora as a kind of female Jesus. Letter to Frederikka Limnell, 17 February 1880, in Lotten Dahlgren, *Lyran* (Stockholm, 1913), p. 316.

5. Erich Wulffen, *Ibsens Nora vor dem Strafrichter und Psychiater* (Halle, 1907). The essay on Nora by Hermann J. Weigand in his *The Modern Ibsen* (New York, 1925), is equally perceptive. On Nora as definitely the hysterical type, who lies pathologically, suppresses her emotions, and suffers from bad traits inherited from her father, see Dr Robert Geyer, *Etude médico-psychologique sur le théâtre d'Ibsen* (Paris, 1902), pp. 37–39.

6. Letter to Olga Knipper, 25 October 1903.

7. Shaw, *Our Theatres in the Nineties* (Standard Edition, London, 1932), III, p. 128.

8. Le Comte Prozor, Introduction to *Le Petit Eyolf* (Paris, 1895), p. xxv. Also in Prozor, 'Ibsen's "Lille Eyolf,"' *Ord och Bild*, IV (1895), p. 370.

"The Land without Paradise"

FIGUREN: Husk at *én* med flamme-riset
mannen drev av paradiset!
Porten har han lagt et sluk for;—
over *det* du springer ei!
BRAND: Åpen lot han *lengslens* vei! (II, 123)

THE FIGURE: Remember, *one* with flaming sword
Drove man out from Paradise!
Outside its gate he set a chasm . . .
Over *that* you will never leap!
BRAND: But he left open the path of *longing*! (III, 246)

This passage, which appears towards the end of *Brand*, contains nearly every feature of the spiritual geography, the mythology and the metaphors which characterise Ibsen's vision of man's fallen state: 'paradiset', the dream of Paradise—that image of a perfectly ordered reality, a model of absolute value, timeless and therefore exempt from the law of change; 'et sluk', an abyss—the real world in which man is mired, exiled from Eden, and subject to process and mutability;[1] 'flamme-riset', the rod of flames—icon of punishment, and a reminder that the wages of sin in the fallen world is death; and 'lengslens vei', the path of longing—man's nostalgic yearning for a lost

From *"Ibsen the Romantic": Analogues of Paradise in the Later Plays*, pp. 9–33. Published by the University of Georgia Press. Copyright © 1982 by Errol Durbach.

Paradise, the source of the Romantic *Sehnsucht* which permeates Ibsen's world like a threnody of loss. The same note sounds again at the end of *Peer Gynt* when, with the eyes of a dying Moses, Peer gazes on a Promised Land which his own experience has turned to dust and ashes. *Lengslens vei* seems no longer open to this death-infected exile from Eden:

> PEER. . . . I'll clamber up to the highest peak;
> I would see the sun rise once again,
> And stare at the promised land till I'm tired;
> Then heap the snow over my head.
> They can write above it: Here lies No one;
> And afterwards—then—! Things must go as they will.
>
> CHURCHGOERS [*singing on the forest path*]:
> Blest morning,
> When God's might
> Spears earth with burning light:
> We, the inheritors,
> Sing out to heaven's towers
> The Kingdom's battle-cry against the night.
> PEER [*crouching in fear*]:
> Don't look that way! It's all a desert.
> Alas, I was dead long before I died. (III, 418)

These lines will re-echo in John Gabriel Borkman's dying vision of another vast and inexhaustible kingdom, 'The Kingdom I was about to take possession of when . . . when I died' (VIII, 231). Like Peer's *lovede land*, Borkman's *rige* is a wilderness of ice and freezing winds; but the crucial difference between these two visions of a ruined and forfeited Eden is that in the later play those contrapuntal, hymn-like reassurances of a Paradise regained all fall silent: the churchgoers' confident belief in *Gudsriket*, the Kingdom of God; their faith as *arvinger*, heirs to a living tradition; and the efficacy of *Gudsrikets tungemål*, the language of God's Kingdom. In Borkman's world there are no such defences against the night and the failure of promise. The protagonists of the later plays now yearn for Paradise in a language which transforms God's *tungemål* into the prose of secular speech; the kingdom for which they yearn is a mundane analogue of some dimly remembered *Gudsrike*; but their yearning seems to intensify in proportion to the steadily diminishing faith that once guaranteed the recovery of Paradise.

Lengslens vei, the Romantic longing for 'Paradise'—whatever the specific, variant meanings of that concept—clearly derives from the mythology of Christian faith and persists, even when that faith declines, in secular expressions of what George Steiner has called a 'deep-seated nostalgia for the absolute'.[2] As many literary historians have argued, the myths of Romanticism and its characteristic concepts appear, both originally and in their later manifestations as 'metareligions' or 'surrogate creeds',[3] 'displaced and reconstituted theology, or else a secularized form of devotional experience'.[4] Marx's dream of a secular Utopia, Freud's vision of a homecoming to death, and Lévi-Strauss's analysis of man's devastation of the last vestiges of Eden are all, in a sense, modern forms of Romanticism; for, as Steiner argues,

> the major mythologies constructed in the West since the early nineteenth century are not only attempts to fill the emptiness left by the decay of Christian theology and Christian dogma. They are themselves a kind of *substitute theology*. They are systems of belief and argument which may be savagely anti-religious, which may postulate a world without God and may deny an afterlife, but whose structure, whose aspirations, whose claims on the believer, are profoundly religious in strategy and in effect.[5]

One version of Ibsen's Romanticism is clearly that of a secular theodicy, a response to man's need for consolation against the certainty of death in a world no longer able to assuage his fears, the need to redeem the consequences of the Fall by a powerful assertion of the imagination, and the need to rediscover godhead in the God-abandoned universe.

I

It is a basic premise in Ibsen's later plays that God is dead. One tends to take this fact for granted, relegating the drama to that general cultural climate defined by Hillis Miller in *The Disappearance of God*, or gesturing vaguely towards Nietzsche's sonorous pronouncement of God's death in *The Joyful Wisdom* of 1882 to account for the habitual failure of faith among Ibsen's protagonists. But, as early as 1866, Brand had already sung the obsequies for the God of a debilitated dispensation—rejecting, as Kierkegaard had before him, 'the impersonation of insipid human kindliness'[6] in the languishing figure of a discredited, post-Enlightenment Christ.

> BRAND: . . . *I* am going to a funeral.
> AGNES: A funeral?
> EINAR: Who's being buried?
> BRAND: The God you just called *yours* . . .
>   The God of hacks and time-serving drudges

Shall be wrapped in his shroud and laid in his coffin.
And in broad daylight. This thing must have an end.
It is time, don't you see? He has been ailing
These thousand years. (III, 88)

The voice of God may still be heard in that ironic declaration of *caritas* as
the avalanche buries Brand. But the central experience of the play remains
His progressive disappearance, implicit in the substitution of materialism for
faith and of bread for belief in the community, the growing secularism of
the Church as a now effete institution, and, paradoxically, in Brand's own
assertion of God's ministry after burying the 'holy decrepitude' of nominal
Christendom. By redefining God in the image of his own intransigent will,
by assuming the mantle of a self-appointed prophet, he stands in the gravest
danger of aspiring towards godhead 'simply to seem worthy' (in the words
of Nietzsche's madman) of filling God's empty space. He rejects the community as unworthy of grace. He sacrifices child, wife and mother to the
deification of his own uncompromising nature. And he imposes on humanity an image of God so relentlessly merciless and cold that his most notable
achievement, as Shaw unkindly puts it, is to have caused 'more intense suffering by his saintliness than the most talented sinner could possibly have
done with twice his opportunities'.[7]

Shaw is unkind because he fails to take account—so much does he
loathe the idealist—of the ambivalence which characterises the Romantic,
or the magnificence of his attempt to restore man 'to the condition in which
he walked with God in the garden'.[8] Brand fails, because he never stops to
inquire whether his call to spiritual revolution derives from the living God or
from some neurotic inner compulsion. Intending the career of a Kierkegaardian knight of faith, Brand finally enacts the arrogance of a Nietzschean super-
man whose God is indistinguishable from the loveless, discreative impulses of
his own personality. And God, so defined, is as good as dead. *Brand* is as complete a rendering of the Nietzschean madness and as critical an analysis of the
Kierkegaardian position as one could hope to find among the statements of
crisis that characterise the spiritual history of the nineteenth century. Ibsen
did not merely allude to the tradition and its horrors, which cliché has already
dulled for us. He dramatised, in a series of extraordinary variations, the means
of God's death and its awful implications for those who live in the abyss.

In the plays that follow *Emperor and Galilean*, the voice of God and the
voices that once chanted His litanies all fall silent, or echo only as parodies of
a remembered liturgy. In the grey Galilean world of *Ghosts* the remnants of
Christian doctrine persist only as moribund ideas—'old defunct theories, all
sorts of old defunct beliefs' (V, 384)—which continue to haunt Mrs Alving.

God has already given way to duty, and dogma to the power of public opinion. And, when human nature rushes in to fill God's empty spaces, it does so not in the effete Christianity of Manders but in Engstrand's specious manipulation of orthodox systems of morality, rationalised in the moral piety that will eventually persuade the Church into partnership with the brothel-keeper. The Devil speaks the language of the priest, and an entire moral system stands upon the verge of collapse. Christian values have become mere ghosts, old virtues emptied of validity, and unscrupulously exploited by hypocrites who can turn the system into profit. Dressed in the piety of his Sunday suit, Engstrand demonstrates the power that feeds off the last tatters of orthodoxy and reduces it to nonsense. He is the repository of all values perverted, and everything eventually passes to him: the power of priesthood, the Alving money, the Alving name, the Alving daughter. It is Engstrand who triumphantly inherits the fallen world.

In *Ghosts* the parody of *Gudsrikets tungemål* is shocking, ironic. In the final scene of *The Wild Duck*, in the desperate attempt of the onlookers to reconcile the death of Hedvig with a tradition of grief that can contain it, the language of prayer passes beyond parody into black and aching farce:

> HJALMAR. . . . [*He clenches his hands and cries to heaven*]:
>   Oh, God in high . . . if Thou *art* there! Why hast Thou done
>   this to me?
> GINA: Hush, hush, you mustn't say such terrible things.
>   We had no right to keep her, I dare say.
> MOLVIK: The child is not dead; it sleeps.
> RELLING: Rubbish! . . .
> MOLVIK [*stretches out his arms and mutters*]: Praised be
>   the Lord. Earth to earth . . . earth to earth . . .
> RELLING [*whispers*]: Shut up, man! You are drunk! (VI,
> 240–1)

The priest who presides over these obsequies is defrocked and drunk—but not so drunk as to forget that poignant account in Mark's gospel of the raising to life of Jairus's daughter: '*Barnet er ikke dødt: det sover*'—'The child is not dead, but asleep. . . . And taking the child by the hand he said to her, "Talitha kum!" which means, "Little girl, I tell you to get up." The little girl got up at once and began to walk about, for she was twelve years old' (Mark 5: 39–43). It is within the perspective of a faith now hopelessly inoperative that Hedvig's absurdly meaningless sacrifice must ultimately be viewed. There is no language, except that of despair, in which to speak of it. And even *that* language is reduced to platitude or pathetic self-indulgence.

It is in *Rosmersholm*, however, that God's disappearance becomes the first term in the protagonists' strenuous moral argument: 'There is no judge over us', Rosmer admits in the spirit of terrible freedom. 'Therefore we must see to it that we judge ourselves' (VI, 379). Existential freedom—man's consciousness of absolute autonomy in the absence of God—imposes upon him the responsibility of exemplary moral action, the imperative to create value where none exists even to the extent of holding a final doom session over the self. But, however their responses are manifested, there is scarcely a major protagonist in any of Ibsen's last plays who does not model his values and behaviour on the assumption of a *deus absconditus* or whose spiritual status is not defined by that awareness. They are either pagan devotees of Dionysos or seekers after the pre-Christian spirit of the ancient Vikings, self-declared apostates or defrocked priests, freethinkers, atheist rebels, or agnostics tormented by their doubt. Hedda dreams of the free spirit, irradiated by the orgastic religion of ancient Greece, living as God amidst the clutter of bourgeois existence. Solness shakes his fist in the face of an apathetic deity who sanctions the senseless deaths of little children, and dedicates himself to a new religion of secular humanism. And Allmers, the self-styled atheist, devotes himself to a momentous existential undertaking, nothing less than the definitive exploration of '*det menneskelige ansvar*'—man's responsibility—under the great stillness of the heavens. But in his dreams he still yearns for the beneficent God who will recreate the malformed world by healing his crippled child, a subconscious clinging to that old habit of mind which cannot easily relinquish the certainty, stability, reassurance and comfort of the Christian dispensation. In many ways Allmers's predicament seems the paradigm of the Romantic dilemma in Ibsen's drama, which, to state it in its simplest and crudest terms, is to be trapped between a traumatic sense of existence as process, change and death in a world devoid of consistent value, and a nostalgic longing for a lost world of static hierarchies where death has no dominion. And in order to resolve this dilemma, the atheist / agnostic / apostate will fashion out of the raw material of existence his analogue of that lost Eden—a symbolic Paradise which promises eternal life, and which he seeks to possess not as *metaphor* but as *fact*.

II

The idea of Paradise as one of the central myths of the Romantic imagination has been illustrated, in its historical variety and complexity, by M. H. Abrams in *Natural Supernaturalism*. The tradition is inaugurated, he suggests, in Wordsworth's revaluation of Milton's theodicy and his redefinition in secular terms of the 'paradise within'. Having lost faith in an apocalypse by revelation, he argues, the Romantics turned to the hope of recovering

Paradise by revolution; and, when the French Revolution failed to realise that political Eden in which man would live as the New Adam, the despair and disillusionment yielded a single solution: a revolution in the spirit of man, an apocalypse by imagination or cognition which would restore heroism to the ordinary, and grandeur to the dimensions of everyday experience.[9] This is the substance of Wordsworth's 'high Romantic argument' in which pre-Christian intimations of a golden age or pastoral Elysium, and Miltonic echoes of a lost Christian Paradise, are all subsumed in the conviction that man's imagination can rediscover, in the natural world, an earthly Paradise rooted in the life of the common man:

> Paradise, and groves
> Elysian, Fortunate Fields—like those of old
> Sought in the Atlantic Main—why should they be
> A history only of departed things,
> Or a mere fiction of what never was?[10]

Man's mind, in harmonious union with nature, makes possible a spiritual redemption from the 'sleep of death'. It rediscovers, in other words, a spiritual value within the otherwise inanimate world of mundane reality with which the self can unite in a great 'consummation'.

The desire for spiritual transformation, for resurrection from the sleep of death into a state of Edenic perfection, finds expression, more or less literally, in nearly all of Ibsen's plays. Its affinity with remembered vestiges of an earlier Christian tradition is particularly evident in Rubek's vision, in *When We Dead Awaken*, of a Paradise regained through the artefacts of the artistic imagination. His great sculptural masterpiece, 'The Day of Resurrection', is the perfect dramatic correlative of the Romantic quest: 'My vision of Resurrection—the loveliest, most beautiful image I could think of—was of a pure young woman, untainted by the world, waking to light and glory, and having nothing ugly or unclean to rid herself of' (VIII, 278). But the 'resurrection' that Rubek desires is possible only *outside* of nature, that unclean and tainted world of the chasm—and only in an immediate reconstitution of the old Paradise in the new without the intervening fall. It may be possible to see a Wordsworthian solution in some aspects of Ibsen's thought; but it is Ibsen's sceptical questioning of that Romantic tradition that ultimately defines his vision. For Ibsen, to discover Paradise as a 'simple produce of the common day'[11] and to find a solution to spiritual death in the radical identity of self and nature, the Romantic protagonist must have had to make two assumptions: that some divine reality must necessarily inhere beneath the surface of phenomenal nature, and that the essential self can discover its analogue

in the epiphany of 'natural supernaturalism'.[12] But in Ibsen's plays, as I have
suggested, nature is no longer instinct with sympathetic Paradisal affinities.
It is a world without value, a desolate reality. The epiphany of light and clarity at the end of *Ghosts*, illuminating a landscape of unremitting harshness, is
an emblem of the tragic fact that joy and glory are no longer discoverable in
the frozen waste beyond the little world of men. 'Man's discerning intellect',
to use Wordsworth's phrase, finds no analogy, in *Ghosts*, with a 'goodly universe';[13] and the Ibsen protagonist who seeks his kingdom in the mountain
world of nature encounters only the brute, indifferent force of the avalanche.
The self, moreover, in Ibsen's world, has no essential ground of value which
finds its counterpart in nature. It is fragmentary, illusory, and it leads those
who seek it out to the 'nothingness' at the core of Peer Gynt's onion.

Again, there is a close association between Ibsen's vision of man's lost
integrity and that of Blake and the German Romantics, who envisage the Fall
from Paradise in images of fragmentation and alienation, and who dream of
a state of self-completion and community in some New Jerusalem or *Drittes
Reich*. The disintegration of the self, the fragmented social order, Blake's 'fall
into Division', Hölderlin's description of society as *disjecta membra*, Hegel's
sense of his culture as 'the self-alienated spirit'[14]—all these images of a fall
from wholeness, and the promise of a Paradise restored, find articulate expression in the visionary speeches of Brand:

> But there is
> One thing that does prevail and endure—
> That is the uncreated spirit, once redeemed
> From Chaos in the first fresh Spring of time, and still
> Extending bridges of unalterable faith
> From banks of flesh to banks of spirit.
> Now it is hawked from door to door, and cheap . . .
> Thanks to this generation's view of God.
> But out of these dismembered wrecks of soul,
> From these truncated torsos of the spirit,
> From these heads, these hands, there shall arise
> A whole being, so that the Lord
> May recognize his creature Man once more,
> His greatest masterpiece, his heir,
> His Adam, powerful, and tall, and young! (III, 92–3)

There are echoes, here, of Blake's Universal Man, the first Adam, who falls
from 'Perfect Unity' and the 'Universal Brotherhood of Eden'[15] into division
and fragmentation, and whose 'Resurrection into Unity' is effected through

a redemptive vision of Paradise where integrity is rediscovered. But Brand locates this new Eden within his own psyche—a reflection of his desire, very like Peer Gynt's, to be 'myself entirely', to seek traditional values not outwards or upwards but in the deep recesses of the self, in this way becoming both subject and source of his own redemptive psychology:

> Within! Within! That is my call!
> That is the way I must venture! That is my path!
> One's own inmost heart—*that* is the world,
> Newly created, and ripe for God's work.
> *There* shall the vulture of the will be slain.
> And *there* shall the new Adam at last be born again. (114–15)

To restore the 'new Adam' in oneself becomes one of the enduring quests, given the notations and the terms of modern existentialism, of Ibsen's protagonists in the later plays—a strenuous attempt to envision new heaven and new earth, the wholly integrated self, by reordering one's processes of consciousness, by *seeing differently*. 'The eye altering alters all', says Blake.[16] But, if the visionary revelation can redeem man by making him whole again, it can also damn him when he sees obliquely with the scratched left eye of the troll. John Gabriel Borkman, in an ironic echo of Blake's aphorism, justifies his vision of a monstrously distorted reality in the language of a romanticism become perverse: 'Det er øyet som forvandler handlingen', he says. 'Det gjenfødte øye forvandler den gamle handling' (III, 550)—'It is the eye that transforms the deed. The eye, regenerated, transforms the old deed.' The source of Romantic salvation, the eye, now blurs the moral and spiritual vision into a form of astigmatism incapable of distinguishing between the new Adam and the old. Neither Brand nor any other of Ibsen's visionary humanists succeeds in finding the 'Perfect Unity' *within*, nor the 'Universal Brotherhood of Eden' in which the entire social community regains its cohesion.

The external corollary to the search within is a paradise of the harmoniously ordered cultural life, in which the antinomies of existence are reconciled in a new spiritual amalgam—those analogues of the Third Empire that recur in so many of the plays after *Emperor and Galilean*, where the idea is most clearly defined. It is not a quintessentially Ibsenian concept, as it is sometimes assumed to be. There are echoes of Kant, Hegel, Schiller and Blake in its formulation;[17] and Wordsworth's divine-poetic mission, his programme for the regeneration of the human spirit in a democracy of souls, has its origins in a similar revelation of the new egalitarian community. Rosmer's vision, in its general implications, is similarly Wordsworthian—an attempt to transcend the conflict of orthodoxy and liberalism, the forces tearing society apart, in a new nobility of mind and soul until the ripples of his idealism, spreading in ever widening circles, finally incorporate one universal nobleman. Borkman's empire of benevolent socialism, Solness's dedication to human happiness in creating homes for men—these visions imply a variation on the 'Universal Brotherhood of Eden'. But there is no Third Empire in Ibsen where all contradiction is finally resolved in Edenic harmony, or where the attempt to synthesise discordant opposites does not result in their mutual destruction. Nor is the humanist ideal of the regenerated community ever realised within the smaller unit of the family; for the idealist himself inevitably proves incapable of sustaining, in his own fragmented and alienated life, the joy and community he so fervently envisions. The fallen world in Ibsen remains a world of division, a *perpetuum mobile* of conflicting impulses which denies the Romantic dream of a reintegrated Eden.

The analogues of Paradise in Romantic and post-Romantic literature are legion; and, even when poets no longer speak of the classical Elysium or the New Jerusalem or Paradise, their secular variants on the happy prelapsarian place remain authentic replications of the Edenic idea. Similarly in Ibsen, although the literal concepts of *Paradis*, *lovede land* or *Gudsrike* are almost entirely obscured beneath the colloquial dialogue of the realistic drama, they are nevertheless invoked by ingenious secular equivalents of Paradise: Hedda's vision of a mythical pagan alternative to bourgeois culture, in which men live in freedom as demigods; John Gabriel Borkman's ore-bearing, subterranean kingdom of infinite riches and power; Solness's airborne Kingdom of Orangia; or, more abstract in its conception, Allmers's search for a dimension of human existence forever exempt from the law of change—Eden as a condition of imperishable angelic bliss. These, and many others, are the kingdoms of power and glory which Ibsen's protagonists try to fashion out of the raw material of human experience. But what Ibsen dramatises in these alternative Edens is the fallibility inherent in *all* the Romantic visions of Paradise—that converse of a vital, positive and spiritually redemptive vision of perfect unity. For just as *lengslens vei*, the longing for Paradise, may finally infect the soul with the sort of *Heimweh* that afflicts Ellida Wangel, so Paradise itself may prove an illusion concealing a barren waste, a mirage hovering above the reality of devastation. This is the ambivalence that Northrop Frye detects in the very structure of Romantic symbolism:

> The journey within to the happy island garden or the city of light is a perilous quest, equally likely to terminate in the blasted ruins of Byron's *Darkness* or Beddoes's *Subterranean City*. In many Romantic poems, including Keats's nightingale ode, it is suggested

that the final identification of and with reality may be or at least include death.[18]

But the most appalling aspect of the quest for Paradise is that it may lead towards an anti-Eden, a world of static forms, of cold and motionless alternatives to human passion and joy—most certainly an ideal world in being exempt from process, but paradoxically dead in its very deathlessness and incapable of accommodating man as living inhabitant. These are the 'cold pastoral' qualities of Keats's Grecian Urn—an alternative to the world of human limitation and the multiple frustrations of 'breathing human passion', but an Eden forever petrified in frozen gestures of unconsummated love, a world out of nature where nothing lives or moves. If it evokes sensations of beauty, this Paradise also invites a complex of unrequited desires to match the frustrations of the phenomenal world. Byzantium, in Yeats's 'Sailing to Byzantium', is another such Paradise sundered from the realities of process which make us human but render us mortal. The most complete analysis of the fallacies of Paradise appears in Wallace Stevens's 'Sunday Morning', with its image of that deathless state for which his persona yearns, but which is merely another aspect of the death she fears. It is a poem which makes fully articulate what is implicit in nearly all the later plays of Ibsen, where to live in the Paradise of one's own construction is to dwell down among the dead men:

> Is there no change of death in paradise?
> Does ripe fruit never fall? Or do the boughs
> Hang always heavy in that perfect sky,
> Unchanging, yet so like our perishing earth,
> With rivers like our own that seek for seas
> They never find, the same receding shores
> That never touch with inarticulate pang?[19]

The self made whole again, the secular guarantee of immortality, a pseudo-religious defence against the fear of death—however one defines the nature of the Paradisal quest, it is clear from Ibsen's analysis of Romantic psychology that the search may lead directly to a living Hell, and that in the very attempt to fashion an alternative Eden the protagonist may destroy the life around him and consign himself to a living death. For if 'Paradise' is their only possible answer in the Godless universe to the ravages of time and the consequences of the Fall, then it must by its very nature be timeless and immutable—like death itself. It is one of the central ironies in Ibsen that the fear of death impels his protagonists towards the morbidity and deadliness which characterise their kingdom—that frozen no man's land 'which never moves, which never changes, which never grows older, but which remains forever, icy and silent.'[20] The ambivalent Paradise of Ibsen's drama, the double vision which perceives it, and the equivocal nature of his Romanticism finally extend to our perception of his protagonists and our evaluation of their life-missions, quests, and ideals—a gallery of magnificent and mad Romantics, whose Edenic visions are the source at once of their potential redemption and their unregenerate destruction.

III

It is not entirely surprising that Ibsen hardly, if ever, appears in histories of European Romantic or post-Romantic literature—a fate he shares with Byron, and probably for much the same reason: 'Byron I omit altogether,' writes M. H. Abrams in his Preface to *Natural Supernaturalism*, 'not because I think him a lesser poet than the others but because in his greatest work he speaks with an ironic counter-voice and deliberately opens a satirical perspective on the vatic stance of his Romantic contemporaries.'[21] Precisely the same may be said of Ibsen the Romantic; and those definitions of Romanticism, such as Morse Peckham's[22] which must bend and twist themselves to accommodate the peculiar genius of Byron also make it possible to read Ibsen in a similar light. Byron, in fact, is one of the few English Romantics whom Ibsen knew (in Adolf Strodtmann's German translation); and his enigmatic comments in a letter of 1872 suggest that Byron assumed an importance for him quite disproportionate to Ibsen's acquaintance with his poetry:

> I have not read very much of Byron, but I have a feeling that his works translated into our language would be of great assistance in freeing our aesthetics from many moral prejudices—which would be a great gain. . . . It is acknowledged here that German literature required Byron's assistance to enable it to reach its present standpoint; and I maintain that we need him to free us from ours.[23]

What Byron he might have read, and how much, is uncertain; and I make no claims for influence. But the voice that cries out in *Cain* re-echoes also in *Hedda Gabler* and *Rosmersholm* and *Little Eyolf*, not merely the ironic counter-voice of a Romantic dissident, but the cry of fear in the face of death and the silence of God—that awareness of what it means to inhabit 'the Land without Paradise'.

'*The Land without Paradise*' is the stage-setting for Byron's *Cain*, one of his typically abstract locations which replace the physical landscape of conventional drama with a dramatic image of man's metaphysical condition. Like the *sluk*, Ibsen's image of the abyss outside the gate of paradise, Byron's is a world in which man must die—the fallen world of process, time and change; and the absurdity of existence under the sentence of death befouls for Cain, as it does for Hedda or Allmers, the very quality of life itself:

> I live
> But to die. And living, see no thing
> To make death hateful, save an innate clinging,
> A loathsome and yet all invincible
> Instinct of life, which I abhor, as I
> Despise myself, yet cannot overcome.
> And so I live. (*Cain*, I. 109–15)

He yearns for Paradise—which, for him, is a condition of eternal life—hating his parents who brought death into the world, estranged from an apathetic God whose morality is merely circumstantial, who can make sin of virtue within a single generation by turning Cain's love for his sister into the flaming rod of punishment for their children. Above all, since death has not yet become a human experience in the Land without Paradise, Cain's fear of what remains mysterious and inexplicable to all men infects his being all the more intensely:

> Thoughts unspeakable
> Crowd in my breast to burning when I hear
> Of this almighty Death, who is, it seems,
> Inevitable. (I. 257–60)

There is no consoling faith for him, nothing to counteract man's final obliteration into nothingness.

Ibsen's *sluk* shares some of the purely metaphysical dimensions of Byron's Land without Paradise, but its geographical location is also spatial or, at any rate, rooted in the concrete and particular world of phenomenal reality: the wasteland of charred stumps and withered leaves in which Peer Gynt is haunted by memories of lost opportunity; the desiccated garden in which Hedda Gabler is trapped and bored; that world of deliquescent organic change, of growth, decay, ineluctable undertows and death which the Allmers inhabit; and even the bourgeois parlours where death enters by doors barred against it—like Borkman's coffin-trap, another frozen pastoral, echoing with the *danse macabre* even while it tries to sustain the illusion of deathlessness. Existence in the *sluk*, bereft of meaning, becomes mere absurd contingency to those who inhabit it. And, tormented by the fear of death, the senseless decay of the body, the meaninglessness of life, Ibsen's people cry out against the futility of all endeavour. Thus Solness and Allmers:

> And now, looking back, what does it all add up to? In fact, I've built nothing. Nor did I really sacrifice anything for the chance to build. Nothing! Absolutely nothing! (VII, 439–40)

> There must be some meaning in it. Life, existence, providence—surely they can't be so utterly meaningless. . . . Perhaps the whole thing is just haphazard. An aimless drifting, like some wrecked and rudderless ship. (VIII, 67)

Nothing, *nichts*, *ingenting*: this is the distinctive quality of existence in the Land without Paradise. 'One sticks one's finger into the soil', writes Kierkegaard, 'to tell by the smell in what land one is: I stick my finger into existence—it smells of nothing.'[24]

Death in all its manifestations broods over Ibsen's world—not merely in stunning, climactic suicides and accidents, but as a slow ineffable process expressed sometimes through metaphor, sometimes as an abstract concept, sometimes in symbolic or almost expressionist devices invested with recognisable human form, sometimes as characters in the terminal stages of a debilitating disease: syphilis, tuberculosis, cancer. Hedda's world, for example, her very house, stinks with the odour of death—her dead father surveying the action like a ghost, the autumnal garden decaying beyond the French windows, oppressive reminders of old Aunt Rina dying off-stage, Løvborg's shocking suicidal mistake, and Hedda's inevitable final gesture; which destroys both herself and her unborn child. And even beyond this world of dying aunts (whom Hedda cannot bear to see or visit) there is the operation of another force that subsumes all individual death. In *Hedda Gabler* Ibsen calls it 'history'—organic process, flux, and decay in all its manifestations from the foetus in the Gabler womb to the disappearance of Gablerism from the cultural map of European society. In *Little Eyolf* the same general vision of the Land without Paradise is abstracted into *forvandlingens lov*, the law of change, which sooner or later each character contemplates as a power to which all passion, the body, and life are eventually subject. Each in his own way tries to deny this law or arrest it by symbolic means, for each (with the possible exception of Asta) views change not as dynamic possibility, but as deterioration and decay. To discover an *unchanging* principle in human existence and human relationships is, for them all, to rediscover Paradise:

RITA: . . . Anyway, everything has to end sometime.

BORGHEJM: Oh, not everything—I hope. . . .

RITA: Not everything, did you say?

BORGHEJM: Yes, I firmly believe that there is at least one thing in this world that has no end.

RITA: You are doubtless thinking of love . . . and similar things.

BORGHEJM: I am thinking of anything which is delightful!

RITA: And which never ends. Yes, let's think of that. And hope for it, all of us. (55)

This sort of yearning, however, is often brutally contradicted by the angels of death who come to remind them of their mortality—such as the Buttonmoulder, waiting for Peer at the next cross-roads; or who, like the Rat Wife and the Stranger from the Sea, embody a conflation of the impulses of sexual love and mortality; or who confront us with the decay of the body not as an abstraction, but as the terrifying reality of sickness and disease, as in the case of Osvald Alving, Dr Rank and Lyngstrand. Ella Rentheim, for example, garbed in black velvet, enters the dark sepulchral world of John Gabriel with the chilling effect of an Ingmar Bergman harbinger of death:

[. . . *The room becomes half dark. A moment later there is a knock on the tapestry-lined door at the back.*]

BORKMAN: Who's that knocking? [*No answer; there is another knock. . . .*] Who is it? Come in!

[ELLA RENTHEIM, *a lighted candle in her hand, appears in the doorway. She is wearing her black dress, as before.*]

BORKMAN [*stares at her*]: Who are you? What do you want with me?

ELLA RENTHEIM [*closes the door and approaches*]: It's me, Borkman. . . . It is 'your' Ella . . . as you used to call me. Once. Many, many years ago. . . . The years have taken a hard toll of me, Borkman. Don't you think so? . . . No longer those dark curls, falling over my shoulders. Remember how you used to love to twist them round your fingers?

BORKMAN [*quickly*]: That's it! I see now. You have changed your hair style. (VIII, 192)

Borkman's reaction to her appearance modulates from a frightened bewilderment to the pathetic, ludicrous, even strangely amusing response of one who—so carefully immured against both life and death—has now to confront the inevitability of change. He simply denies it. Ella's hair, as Ibsen describes it, is 'silver white'—but he responds only to its style and not its colour; she tells him that she is dying of cancer and cannot last the winter—but he reflects that the winters tend to be rather long in Norway. If the fear of change and death compels him to deny the facts, the imminence of death compels Ella towards another solution:

> Think how infinitely sad it is for me to know I shall be taking leave of all living things, of sun and light and air, without leaving behind me a single person who will think of me with affection and sadness, remember me the way a son remembers a mother he has lost. . . . When I die, the name of Rentheim dies too. I feel strangled by the very thought. To be obliterated from existence . . . even to the extent of one's name. . . . Don't let it happen. Let Erhart bear my name after me! (202–3)

Those who die in Ibsen's *sluk* are inevitably the last of their line, so that death comes as total extinction. And the thought of so complete a loss of identity strangles and tortures like the thought that burns in the breast of Cain. Christian assurances of a compensatory Heaven, an afterlife which will confer some ultimate meaning on existence, do not even enter the realm of Ella Rentheim's contemplation. Her answer to death is defiantly secular: she will live on in her surrogate child—not in any literal sense, for he is in fact her sister's son, but in his *perpetuation of her name* as a living idea. *Names*, in this play, assume magical connotations of permanence: imperishable essences which survive mortality, symbols of secular redemption which—like John Gabriel's own pretentious and sonorous name—link the mundane to the archangelic. In the absence of God, Ibsen's protagonists must refashion their own conceptions of divinity; and from the Land without Paradise they must project Edenic denials of the nothingness which confronts them in the end.

The fear of death is not customarily associated with the Romantic temperament, which, we have been habituated to believe, is morbidly *attracted* to the easeful thing rather than fearfully *repelled* by it. Freud's idea of the 'death wish' has set the seal on what is now generally accepted as the Romantic's inherent and instinctive urge towards inertia—as in the case of Werther, the nineteenth-century Hamlet, Keats, and Hedda Gabler, who have all been said to manifest the Freudian syndrome in their search for an alternative to the fallen world. George Steiner puts it well:

> It is the crowning act in Freud's unbroken attempt to reconcile man to a godless reality to make this reality endurable by suggesting

a final release from it.... Whereas Marx intimates an Edenic condition free of necessity and of conflict, Freud knows that such freedom would be tantamount to the repose of death.[25]

But it is precisely against such an Edenic condition that the Ibsen protagonist baulks. Even Hedda, the arch-Romantic, is possessed in equal measure by 'romantic' thoughts of dying beautifully and an overwhelming, 'unromantic' fear of death itself; and it would be more true to say of Ibsen's people that they are defined by a syndrome significantly different from Freud's—by their *refusal to acknowledge* the awful reality of death, and their search for symbols of permanence to counteract that fear. It is a pattern of behaviour most clearly described by Ernest Becker as the *denial of death*: 'The idea of death', he writes, 'the fear of it, haunts the human animal like nothing else; it is the mainspring of human activity—activity designed largely to avoid the fatality of death, to overcome it by denying in some way that it is the final destiny for man.'[26]

This denial, Becker argues, may assume an heroic protest against fate, a life-enhancing illusion which bursts the boundaries of time into a new dimension of reality; or it may manifest itself as a perversion of life, an inability to grasp death as a reality to be acknowledged and transcended. Brand's allegory of the spiritually dead community clinging to memories of the past recalls precisely such perversity. He tells the tale of a king who will not relinquish the corpse of his lover to the grave, incapable of ever admitting the finality of her death, and

> every day undoing
> The patchwork linen of the shroud,
> Putting his ear against the heart,
> And seizing pitiful crumbs of hope
> That life might come again; imagining
> Life's blood-red roses bloomed again
> Upon that clammy form. (III, 239)

Unwilling to face death, he ultimately robs himself of life. And his fate is, in many various ways, the paradigm of all those fear-stricken protagonists in Ibsen who in denying death and questing after permanence commit themselves to death-in-life.

Even Allmers, who more than anyone in Ibsen's plays protests his longing to cease upon the midnight, is patently obsessed by the fear of process and the dread of sexuality. When he speaks of his mountain experience in league with death the good companion—'absolutely without fear' (VIII,

101)—his tone gradually slides into self-indulgent forebodings of mortality which mock their very substance: 'People in my family don't usually live till they are old. . . .' Hermann Weigand, quite correctly, dismisses the whole mountain episode as fabrication, another self-deceiving distortion of fact and feeling: 'In reality he had the worst scare of his life', he writes. 'The hysteria of fright made it appear to him as though death were bodily walking by his side, a gruesome fellow-traveller.'[27] This surely is how death finally appears to Allmers when he comes to claim his child; and it is fear and not fascination that ultimately drives him to the most complex denial of death in Ibsen's drama, to multiple symbols of permanence which assure his special status as a creature somehow exempt from the law of change.

IV

I shall have constantly to return to this triadic pattern in Ibsen's drama—the fear of death, the denial of death, the construction of an elaborate symbol-system to immortalise the self—and, of course, to the paradox which underlies the entire structure and ensures the frustration of the myth of self-perpetuation. As I have suggested, the dominant metaphor of that mythology is the Paradise-kingdom which features so prominently, under a variety of different names—such as Orangia/Appelsinia in *The Master Builder*, or Peer's Gyntiana, which, more consciously than any other of these analogues of Eden, articulates the protagonist's single motivating desire to conquer death:

> The world's outmoded! Now it's the turn
> Of Gyntiana, my new young land!
> Given the capital, it's already done.—
> A golden key to the gate of the ocean!
> A crusade against Death! (III, 345)

Like Borkman's Kingdom, Gyntiana will conquer death in visions of capital and gold, economic imperialism, and those myths of a commercial Paradise which remain the substance of the modern dream—like Gatsby's, and which, like Gatsby's myth, transforms itself into an image of the ash-pit. But the fallible Paradise, the anti-Eden which ultimately exhibits the very qualities of the condition it seeks to elude, is only *one* variation on this Romantic theme. 'Korstog mot døden' (II. 184)—the crusade against death—outlines the nature of the primary, obsessive quest in Ibsen, but not the death-defying strategies of his protagonists. A geographically located 'kingdom' is one such device, but there are so many synonyms for Paradise and so many symbols employed in the crusade, that the geographical metaphor becomes too limiting and narrow. In speaking of 'analogues of Paradise' I also have in mind what Jerome Buckley, in a wide-ranging article, has defined as 'Symbols of Eternity: The Victorian Escape from Time'.[28] His detailing of this pervasive post-Romantic theme offers diverse examples of nineteenth-century Edens, establishing in the particular images of writers from Coleridge to Joyce all the major variants which *cohere* in the drama of Ibsen: Rossetti's 'substitute religion' of sexual experience; the Aesthetic belief in the 'power of art to arrest the moment'; William Morris's attempt, in *The Earthly Paradise*, to fashion 'worlds of artifice beyond the reach of change'; the related attempts of Wordsworth, Pater and Joyce to 'fulfill the desire for everlastingness, for a continuity beyond both sense and time' in moments of epiphany; and Browning's image of Heaven as a 'perpetual extension of his life's unfulfilled mission'. To these symbols of eternity Ibsen adds the peculiar secular and psychic visions that define his own dramatic characters: the self-immortalising myths of Hedda Gabler and John Gabriel Borkman, the chorus of children pressed into the service of an impossible teleological ideal, and sexual desire divinised by taboo into forms of the imperishable. None of these human realities survives the process of Edenic transformation. The self congeals; the child dies; desire remains eternally frustrated. The importance of Ibsen to the history of Romantic ideas, it seems to me, derives from his relentless reappraisal of Romanticism's attempt to deal with the fears and anxieties of existence, his analysis of the failure of substitute religions to assuage the human wound; and, in so far as his vision is powerfully critical in its diagnosis of the fallacies and fallibilities of Romanticism, its characteristic voice will seem correspondingly despairing. But it is not, for this reason, necessarily anti-Romantic.

Morse Peckham has called these phases of disillusionment and despair in nineteenth-century literature 'Negative Romanticism' and its alienated and guilt-ridden spokesman the 'Byronic hero'—terms challenged by those for whom Romanticism is an essentially affirmative tradition, and for whom a heroism based upon negation would be anathema. M. H. Abrams, in rejecting the 'counter-Romantic' voice as heretical or renegade, would seem to assume this position. But, however questionable his terms of reference, Morse Peckham does provide the context of ideas and movements to which Ibsen's anomalous romanticism belongs. He argues, moreover, that 'Negative Romanticism' (Carlyle's 'Everlasting No', for example, or Byron's nihilism) is merely a precondition for the positive recovery of meaning in the Godless post-Enlightenment universe.[29] And, however misguided the methods of Ibsen's Romantic questors, their search for value remains the positive corollary of their devastation of *all* value in the attempt. What the plays reveal is the difficulty and the pain of the search for value, the ceaseless probing, the strenuous experimental attempts to grasp the nature of reality, the tragedy of living through the intermediate phases of despair between the loss of Paradise and its rediscovery. Ibsen's romanticism, embodied in the world of his drama, is a process of constructive evolution through which the mind and spirit of man moves: from the collapse of Enlightenment values and the death of God, through vain and self-defeating attempts to insulate the self against absurd contingency, discovering—sporadically and intermittently—a resolution of the Romantic dilemma in what we now recognise as an existential reshaping of man's moral nature and his spiritual wholeness. And, if the vision seems peculiarly 'counter-Romantic', 'negative' or despairing in its analysis of error, it is also guardedly optimistic in its view of man—a challenge to the modern sensibility, whose psychology and symbols remain predominantly Romantic, to formulate constructive responses to traumatic experience without recourse to glib despair. If the 'counter-Romantic' voice instructs by negative example, by irony, there is also that other voice that celebrates joy in the jaws of death, that sees in the law of change not decay but the continuous transformation of the self, that re-establishes value in an empty world by accepting responsibility for one's actions and decisions, and that creates meaning in the void where none existed.

I do not see Ibsen's drama as a *consistent* or *coherent* movement from despair to resolution, or from Negative Romanticism to existentialism; nor do I share Brian Johnston's sense of a programmatic Hegelian development in his plays. The evolution of mind and spirit, bedevilled by incomprehension, occasionally discovering in 'responsibility' or 'joy' a possible way out of its dilemma, now plunging into chaos again when such solutions seem inadequate or inappropriate to the psychic needs of the character—it is this ebb and flow that seems to characterise the rhythm of Ibsen's romanticism. It is not my intention, therefore, to follow any chronological method in discussing the plays—nor, indeed, to offer thoroughly comprehensive analyses in the excellent style of John Northam or Charles Lyons. I have offered here a general model of the Romantic dilemma, the crises of faith which precipitate it, the anxieties which are their consequence, and the metaphors and symbols which link Ibsen's specific vision of the dilemma to the larger context of English and European Romanticism.

NOTES

1. These two aspects of Ibsen's symbol-system have been discussed in illuminating detail by Charles Lyons in *Henrik Ibsen: The Divided Consciousness* (Carbondale and Edwardsville, Ill., 1972). He sees them primarily as opposing myths of order and the chaos of phenomenal existence (to which all order ultimately reverts), and, like many critics of Ibsen's mythology, he emphasises the esoteric and peculiar nature of these symbols. 'Ibsen', he writes, 'is concerned with myth, but his concern is with private processes of consciousness, not with racial or communal patterns of action' (p. xiii). I would argue that the Paradise-abyss mythology in Ibsen

links the psychological anxieties of the individual to a pervasive and public pattern of action.

2. George Steiner, *Nostalgia for the Absolute* (Toronto, 1974) p. 5.

3. Ibid., p. 2.

4. M. H. Abrams, *Natural Supernaturalism*, p. 65.

5. Steiner, *Nostalgia*, p. 4.

6. From Søren Kierkegaard, *Attack upon 'Christendom'* (1854–5), trs. W. Lowrie (Princeton, NJ, 1944) p. 123.

7. *Shaw and Ibsen: Bernard Shaw's 'The Quintessence of Ibsenism' and Related Writings*, ed. J. L. Wisenthal (Toronto, 1979) p. 133.

8. Ibid., p. 137.

9. Abrams, *Natural Supernaturalism*, ch. 6 (pp. 325–72).

10. William Wordsworth, 'Prospectus for "The Recluse"', ll. 47–51. See Abrams, *Natural Supernaturalism*, p. 467.

11. Wordsworth, 'Prospectus for "The Recluse"', l. 55.

12. Morse Peckham discusses the fallibility of these assumptions as 'Analogism' in *Romanticism: The Culture of the Nineteenth Century* (New York, 1965) pp. 25–6.

13. Wordsworth, 'Prospectus for "The Recluse"', ll. 52–3.

14. See Abrams, *Natural Supernaturalism*, pp. 257–8, 293.

15. Ibid., p. 256.

16. Ibid., p. 375.

17. See ibid., p. 206 for a discussion of Kant's 'higher third stage'—a synthesis of nature and culture.

18. Northrop Frye, 'The Drunken Boat: The Revolutionary Element in Romanticism', in Frye (ed.), *Romanticism Reconsidered* (New York and London, 1963) p. 19.

19. Wallace Stevens, 'Sunday Morning', from *The Palm at the End of the Mind* (New York, 1971) p. 7.

20. Harold Pinter, *No Man's Land* (London, 1975) p. 95.

21. Abrams, *Natural Supernaturalism*, p. 13.

22. See Peckham, *Romanticism*, and 'Toward a Theory of Romanticism', *PMLA*, LXVI (1951) 5–23.

23. *Ibsen: Letters and Speeches*, ed. Evert Sprinchorn (New York, 1964) p. 118.

24. Kierkegaard, quoted in J. Hillis Miller, *The Disappearance of God* (Cambridge, Mass., 1963) p. 9.

25. Steiner, *Nostalgia*, p. 21.

26. Ernest Becker, *The Denial of Death* (New York, 1973) p. ix.

27. Hermann Weigand, *The Modern Ibsen* (New York, 1925) pp. 342, 344.

28. Jerome Buckley, 'Symbols of Eternity: The Victorian Escape from Time', in Warren D. Anderson and Thomas D. Clareson (eds), *Victorian Essays: A Symposium* (Kent, Ohio, 1967) pp. 1–15. The quotations that follow derive from this source.

29. See Peckham, *Romanticism, and Beyond the Tragic Vision: The Quest for Identity in the Nineteenth Century* (New York, 1962).

30. Quoted by Abrams, *Natural Supernaturalism*, p. 416. Baudelaire is referring, here, to the artificial paradise induced by drugs.

JAMES WALTER MCFARLANE

Drama and the Person: An Enemy of the People; The Wild Duck; Rosmersholm

It was Georg Brandes who suggested that much of *An Enemy of the People* (1882), *The Wild Duck* (1884), and *Rosmersholm* (1886) might be traced to a point of common origin: the hurt, the distress and disgust Ibsen felt at the hostile reception given in 1881 by the Norwegian public and critics to *Ghosts*. Within a year of this bitterly resented publication, Ibsen had given his answer to those who had abused him: a play (actually begun before *Ghosts* but now splendidly appropriate to the new situation) which traces the bewilderment and incredulity and ultimate exasperation of one who, for publishing unpalatable truths about the polluted sources of the community's economy, is subjected to insult and slander and even physical violence from his fellows. After thus venting his immediate anger, Ibsen in his next play allowed himself a second and more searching look at this phenomenon of a man who makes it his mission to proclaim truth; and *The Wild Duck*, in asking whether it really does add to the sum total of human happiness to put the average person in possession of the truth, redresses a balance. The tertiary stage of exasperation was reached with *Rosmersholm*, a further exploration of the theme of one whose dementia was truth, who like his earlier counterparts had improving designs on his fellows, but whose ultimate achievement is equally unavailing, though not in the same way and not for the same reasons.

From *Ibsen & Meaning: Studies, Essays & Prefaces 1953–87*, pp. 251–71. Published by Norvik Press. Copyright © 1989 by James McFarlane.

Comparable though the three plays may be in this particular respect, they nevertheless vary greatly in quality. *An Enemy of the People* generally ranks as one of the thinnest of Ibsen's maturer works, one which, to use William Archer's phrase, is 'not so richly woven, not as it were, so deep in pile'. Archer goes on: 'Written in half the time Ibsen usually devoted to a play, it is an outburst of humorous indignation, a *jeu d'esprit*, one might almost say, though the *jeu* of a giant *esprit*. . . . *An Enemy of the People* is a straightforward spirited melody; *The Wild Duck* and *Rosmersholm* are subtly and intricately harmonized.' The two latter plays are often to be observed in the critics' estimates vying with each other as rivals for the top place among Ibsen's works: Nils Kjaer's characterization of *The Wild Duck* as 'the master's masterpiece' has been echoed many times in the critical studies of recent decades; and it is repeatedly claimed on behalf of *Rosmersholm* that never was Ibsen's constructional skill more confidently or more successfully exploited.

To plot these three dramas against the co-ordinates of technique and ultimate meaning provides evidence, however, of something more than the mere amplification, or even enrichment, of things already there in essence at the beginning; it is to testify also, and more importantly, to a distinct turning-point in Ibsen's authorship, a change of direction arguably no less profound and no less significant than his earlier abandonment of verse as the medium of his dramas in favour of prose. As a rule it was only with the greatest reluctance that Ibsen was ever drawn to comment on his own work; his letters to his publisher and to his friends tended to harden into a drily formal, almost communiqué-like phraseology whenever it was a question of reporting progress on his own work: a bare admission that he was busy, a hint of whether or not the thing had a contemporary theme, a forecast of the number of acts it would be in, and (for his publisher) perhaps an estimated time for completion, or some indication of the number of printed pages it would fill. Rarely was there anything else of much significance. It is precisely this habitual uncommunicativeness that makes his unsolicited comment on *The Wild Duck* the rather startling thing it is: writing to his publisher on 2 September 1884, he was moved to admit that he thought of this new work of his as something rather special, adding that his methods were new, and that some of the country's younger dramatists might possibly be encouraged by them to launch out along new tracks. It is therefore not without a certain measure of approval from Ibsen himself that one is tempted to consider *An Enemy of the People* as the culmination of a distinct 'period' in the dramatist's career, as something that set a terminus to the line of the development that had begun with *Pillars of Society* in 1877, and had continued by way of *A Doll's House* (1879) and *Ghosts* (1881). There is encouragement also to see *Rosmersholm* as the inauguration of the later mode of composition serving the group of plays that marked the end of his career: *The Lady from the Sea* (1888), *Hedda Gabler* (1890), *The Master Builder* (1892), *Little Eyolf* (1894), *John Gabriel Borkman* (1896), and *When We Dead Awaken* (1899). And—intractable, transitional, between two 'periods'—*The Wild Duck*, composed at a time when its author's dramatic credo was profoundly changing.

* * *

The pace of *An Enemy of the People* is unusual for Ibsen; elsewhere, at least in the later dramas, the progression is purposefully deliberate, like an exploratory advance over uncertain country which has had careful preliminary study but no close reconnaissance. In this play, by contrast, the advance is conducted with eager exuberance, moving over ground familiar as it might be from regular patrol activity, and not seeming to care greatly if on occasion it happens to put a foot wrong. Part of the terrain had in fact been one of Ibsen's favourite stamping-grounds for over ten years, if not longer: a hatred, carefully nurtured in correspondence and in conversation, of anything in the way of party or association or society or indeed any identifiable grouping that went in for 'majority' practices, that invited majority decisions or accepted majority rule. As early as 1872, he had even talked enthusiastically about undermining the whole concept of statehood, asserting that 'the state is the curse of the individual'. Such political sympathies as he had at the time were reserved for nihilists and anarchists and the extreme left-wing, from a feeling that they at least cared about the big things in life and honestly strove to realize their ideals, whilst the larger parties with their mass appeal struck him as trafficking in nothing but sham and humbug. Organized Liberalism he considered freedom's worst enemy.

To these convictions, the events of the year 1881—the hostile reception given to *Ghosts*—brought peculiar reinforcement. To his scorn of organized politics was now added a consuming contempt for the press, especially the so-called Liberal press. Ibsen was confirmed in his view that the press as then constituted was no better than a parasite on a grotesque and deformed body politic, for ever talking about freedom, but terrified of the realities of it, for ever proclaiming independence although itself merely the slave of public opinion and organized pressure-groups and its own circulation figures.

Three items, chiefly, 'seeded' his mind, super-saturated as it was by bitterness and contempt for these things; and they provided the nuclei around which the drama eventually crystallized. One was an anecdote, reported to him by a German acquaintance, Alfred Meissner, about a spa doctor who had been persecuted by his fellow-townsmen for reporting, to the great detriment of the tourist trade, a local case of cholera. Another was the incident in

February 1881 involving a chemist called Harald Thaulow and the Christiana Steam Kitchens, in which Thaulow was prevented at a public meeting from reading his indictment of the management of the Kitchens and instead delivered an impromptu speech of denunciation. And the third was the personality of his great contemporary Bjørnstjerne Bjørnson.

The life-long relationship between these two men was marked by almost every emotion and attitude except indifference. Never was Ibsen, the self-sufficient, introverted exile, able for long to put out of his mind the image of the popular, rhetorical, extroverted Bjørnson. His feelings were always mixed—admiration, contempt, envy, exasperation, gratitude, affection, resentment, with sometimes one thing preponderating, and sometimes another. At the time Ibsen was working on *An Enemy of the People*, he had cause to think of Bjørnson with gratitude, particularly for the latter's spirited defence of *Ghosts*; and the courage, the bluff honesty, and the fundamental decency that he acknowledged in Bjørnson reappear also in his created hero, Dr. Stockmann.

But the piquancy of the situation can surely not have been lost on the author. Ibsen *à la* Bjørnson! The opportunities were too good to be missed. And there, accompanying his quite genuine regard and affection for his hero, one finds a good deal of dry mockery, directed in particular against Dr. Stockmann's simple-minded, self-opinionated interpretation of things. (One must beware, of course, of ascribing all Stockmann's traits to Bjørnson or even to what Ibsen might have wanted to pin on Bjørnson—the relevance is to be found rather in the author's implicit attitude to his created character, and not in the details.) Dr. Stockmann does not find it easy to relate the immediate problem to any wider context of things; his strength and his weakness lie in his simple directness, his inability to see more than one side of the question; and his brother's remonstrance that the alleged pollution cannot be regarded in isolation as a merely scientific matter but is also political and economic, is not without justification. He lacks any deeper understanding of the motives of human conduct and is even perhaps too easily misled about his own. It is no coincidence that both Stockmann and Gregers have spent much of their adult lives in remote parts, the former stuck away in Arctic Norway as a doctor, and the latter brooding 'up at the works' in Høidal for fifteen years; their conduct lacks the corrective of the 'reality principle', that which could tell them what may be presumed socially possible, and what may not.

It is precisely these temperamental and very human weaknesses in the main character, however, that prevent the drama from degenerating into a theatrical tract; and Ibsen was able to make his Kierkegaardian points about the need for individual decision, the necessity for individual responsibility, and the value of individual courage—especially the courage of one's convictions—and to enlist the sympathies of the audience unambiguously on the side of the lone champion without at the same time making him too offensively virtuous. Against his hero, Ibsen marshals an alliance of vested interest, political hypocrisy, and editorial opportunism: the Mayor, the influential representative of entrenched authority, not without courage of a kind and horribly experienced in the manipulation of others by veiled threat and the promise of favour, who masks self-interest and self-preservation as 'the common good'; Aslaksen, embodying the inherent timidity of public opinion, and making a virtuous 'moderation' out of his essential servility; and Hovstad, hawking his influence to the highest bidder. These are the elements that determine the ultimate shape of the drama, in which principles are balanced against expediency, integrity weighed against quick profits, and the 'individual' involved in a fight against what Hebbel was inclined to call the Idea—the reaction of those who wish to maintain the *status quo* and the inertia and the intolerance of the undifferentiated masses who are their dupes.

* * *

Among the earliest jottings preliminary to *The Wild Duck* are two which make special reference to the business of growing up, the transition from childhood to adulthood: one of them compares the advance of civilization to a child's growing up, whereby instinct is weakened, the power of logical thought is developed, and 'the ability to play with dolls' is lost; the other draws a parallel between the revisionary changes in man's attitude to his past achievements and the way in which a child mind is absorbed into the adult spirit. This manifest interest in the phenomenon of childhood and its advance to maturity was not without its personal side. In 1881 Ibsen had begun a short autobiographical account which, however, never got beyond a description of the days of his earliest childhood in Skien. One can nevertheless well imagine how his memories of those days were jogged by this exercise: of his sister Hedvig; of his father who suffered the shame of bankruptcy and who reduced a once prosperous family to something near penury; of the attic at Venstøp (a few miles out of Skien) where the Ibsen family subsequently lived; of the furniture there and the books and the other old lumber left by a previous occupant; and of the puppet theatre, with which as a boy he had been in the habit of devising little entertainments for family and friends. Particular details like these can easily be picked out as having contributed to *The Wild Duck* in fairly obvious ways; but the more reflective items in the preliminary notes about childhood and its problems count perhaps for even more.

One way of looking at *The Wild Duck* is to see it as a dramatic commentary on the shock of growing up. The Ekdal household, seen as an entity, enjoys an innocent and child-like happiness until this is upset by its introduction, through the agency of Gregers, to a new and disturbing awareness; it gives an account of the thoughtless, brutal imposition of a new and demanding consciousness upon a ménage totally unprepared to face it, and of the sad consequences; it presents a history of shattered illusions and the destruction of make-believe, an account of what happens when a family's 'ability to play with dolls'—or as Relling puts it, its 'life-lie'—is destroyed.

Its most literal representative of childhood is, of course, Hedvig. Standing fearfully yet expectantly on the threshold of adulthood, taking a secret delight in playing with fire, she has all the genuine imaginativeness of the child, and a naïve and still active sense of mystery; responding intuitively to language's more magical powers, she is greatly impressionable and pathetically sensitive to the moods of those about her. Her death is the consequence of her being caught up in the emotional entanglements of an adult world, the result of confused loyalties; and the senselessness of her self-sacrifice and the pity of her fate are things that the drama is particularly concerned to communicate. Balancing her in the composition of the piece is Old Ekdal, who also enjoys 'the ability to play with dolls', but in his case it is the ability of one who has reached a second childhood; he enjoys dressing-up, wearing his old uniform for private and family celebrations; his enthusiasm for the surrogate reality of the attic is genuine and unassumed; helped on occasion by the brandy bottle, he can live himself without difficulty into a world of his own imagining; and his sad and—by its rather touching ridiculousness—moving presence is also an important ingredient in the whole. Between them is Hjalmar. Between the representatives of nonage and dotage, between the embodiments of the puerile and the senile is this defining figure of childishness: a child without the innocence or the sensitivity of a child, a big baby, sometimes petulant and querulous, sometimes appealing and charming, happy to let himself be spoilt by the attentions of others, skilled in tantrum but quite ready (as Hedvig knows) to be distracted by some little treat or favourite toy, by a bottle of beer or his flute. He takes refuge from the disappointments and frustrations of life in daydreams of worldly success, of clearing the family name, which provide him with a kind of substitute purposefulness. He too retains something of 'the ability to play with dolls', but it is a self-conscious, a less wholeheartedly spontaneous thing than that of Hedvig or his father; so that when he uneasily shows the loft and its contents to Gregers, he is quick to shelter behind the excuse that it is for the old man's sake.

What the drama emphasizes is that, before the coming of Gregers, this household was a generally happy one, the members of which had succeeded in amalgamating reality and dream, in bringing them both under one roof as they had conjoined their prosaic studio with their fantastic attic. Access from

the one to the other was just too easy. What they do not at this stage realize is that the relative stability of their world depends on Werle's unobtrusive
manipulations and the cynical adjustments of Relling. These two are the people
in ultimate control, secretly supplying both the worldly goods and the stuff
of fantasy without which life *chez* Ekdal would be impossible. Hidden sub-
ventions provide the material means to bear reality, inspired suggestions sustain their dream-life. That the Ekdals in return help to satisfy some craving or
need in the lives of those who thus manipulate them—serving, one imagines,
self-interest or conscience or cynicism or a sense of secret power—is a further
integral though subsidiary element in the drama. What is important is that
a balanced existence is contrived for the whole family unit, permitting all its
members to fulfil themselves as completely as ever they are likely to. This existence is brought into a state of violent unbalance by the arrival of Gregers, who,
seeing or suspecting something of the conspiracy that thus controls the Ekdals,
feels that he has a duty to expose it; applying a moral imperative, he sets out to
reveal what he regards as the dishonesty inherent in the whole situation.

Like Hjalmar, Gregers gains extra definition in the play from two flank-
ing characters: his father Haakon Werle and Relling. To the former he stands
in contrast by virtue of his lack of practical sense, his alienation from life as
it is really lived; fifteen years in the backwoods is set against the father's successful business career at the centre of things; his inability even to light his
own stove gives heightened emphasis to the quietly purposeful way his father,
with his sure grasp of opportunity and his *savoir faire*, has organized his own
life and the lives of so many of those around him. With Relling—the soul of
cynicism, a maker of dreams for all but himself, whose only solution for his
own problems is a good binge—the contrast is on the plane of idealism. He
takes his fellows firmly by the arm, and beguiling them with pleasant fictions,
leads them quietly away from their own frustrations and the jagged edges of
reality; Gregers, by contrast, rubs their noses in the truth. Gregers represents
what Ibsen had by now rejected—the principle of making universal demands
regardless of person or situation or circumstance. He is the self-elected agent
of his fellows' betterment, trafficking in truth and liberty without any sense of
what is appropriate, or of what allowances to make: liberty, wrote Ibsen in one
of the preliminary notes, 'consists in giving the individual the right to liberate
himself, each according to his personal needs'. Gregers's approach is based on
an inflexibly abstract view of life, a theorist's; wanting the best for his fellows,
and convinced of their power to achieve it by heroic methods, he blunders in
with his missionary fervour and upsets what he does not understand. Human
kind, he fails to realize, cannot bear very much reality.

The compositional pattern of *The Wild Duck* thus poses two figures *en
face*, Hjalmar and Gregers, each with his two supporting figures: Hedvig and

Old Ekdal for the one, and Werle and Relling for the other. But to resolve what would otherwise be merely a dramatic encounter into a dramatic situation, there are cross-references and cross-tensions. Werle is linked to the Ekdal household by former business association and (through Gina) by illicit relations and a suspected paternity; Relling is attached to the Ekdals by his tenancy and daily association, to Gregers by earlier acquaintance up at the works; both are tenuously related to each other through Mrs. Sørby, and so on. The result is a plexus of intimacies, affinities, bonds, transactions, intrusions, importunities. It was perhaps to dispose these elements more eloquently and to control them more effectively that Ibsen seems to have been particularly concerned during the preliminary stages with what one might reasonably call 'depth', a certain quality of perspective. The drafts show how some characters were brought much nearer the foreground, others were stood back, and some even (like Old Ekdal's wife, for instance) taken out of the composition altogether. Then there were others whose actual location seems to have remained very largely unchanged yet whose focus was altered—like the three guests at Werle's party who were originally *named* characters and then later became anonymously typed; or like Mrs. Sørby who in the first mention was an unnamed middle-aged woman. Hand in hand with this went a certain reduction in the definition of what was supplied to the composition by past event; facts in the final version are not things to prove or determine or demonstrate, there is no concern to annex certainty, but instead the design is built up by hint, allusion, suggestion or obliquity generally: Hedvig's paternity, Ekdal's alleged crime, Werle's treatment of his former wife, all these things are deliberately blurred in the interests of the design as a whole. Nor must one forget the extra quality of 'depth' that the language is made to sustain, the loading of it with extra and secretly shared significance, as when Gregers talks to Hedvig.

Finally, is it perhaps in some such terms that the Wild Duck itself is best explained; as something arbitrarily interposed, which additionally to its function in the drama as one of the 'Requisiten' serves also to make more explicit the relationship of the other elements in 'depth'. Because it is not difficult in the circumstances to imagine a *human* reaction without it, it gives the impression of being inserted; what really integrates it into the play is the realization that no genuinely *dramatic* reaction is possible without it. Part of its effect on the play is comparable with that produced by the traditional dramatic unities: it concentrates, it holds together a number of otherwise separate things, it permits that density by which art distinguishes itself from the more diffuse nature of life, it helps to compose the drama. To call it a 'symbol', however, is possibly to emphasize unduly the similarity of the many disparate things it is successively made to stand for: Hedvig, in its role as gift from Werle to the

Ekdals; Old Ekdal, whom life has winged and who has forgotten what real life is like; Hjalmar, who has dived down deep into the mud; Gregers, who suggests that he too will soon accustom himself to his new surroundings; or the object of Gregers's mission, the thing he will, like some extraordinarily clever dog, save from the depths. It is not so much that there is some kind of identity which all these things share, there is no 'falling together' such as the etymology of 'symbol' might suggest; rather it is that the Wild Duck is at the point of convergence of a series of comparisons, the purpose of which is to enable the onlooker to discriminate among the things it serves, to sort them out rather than heap them together, and ultimately to place them in perspective. What happens is that a number of characters are moved to say, or think, or unconsciously propose: 'This or that or he or she equals the Wild Duck', so that the Wild Duck functions almost like a recurrent element in a series of simultaneous metaphorical equations about life and the living of it, a kind of 'x' quality for which a whole range of variables might be substituted in an effort to find some kind of answer to things. Express your answer (the drama seems to enjoin from those who are tempted to try to solve such problems) in terms of truth and human happiness, and comment on the degree of incompatibility indicated.

*   *   *

One of the contributory sources of *Rosmersholm* was undoubtedly Ibsen's disappointment following his first visit to Norway for eleven years. When in the late spring of 1885 he left Italy for Norway, it was not without the hope that he might find life there congenial enough to make him want to settle; but after only four months he was away again to Munich, sickened by too many of the things he had seen and heard to want to stay in the North. 'Never have I felt more alienated by the *Tun und Treiben* of my Norwegian compatriots than after the lessons they read me last year', he wrote to Georg Brandes in November 1886. 'Never more repelled. Never more discomfited.' Many of the less admirable qualities pilloried in *Rosmersholm* have their origin in this sense of repulsion: the cruel fanaticism of Kroll, whom Ibsen created to represent extreme right-wing thought in Norway; the sacrifice of principles to expediency and party advantage that the left-wing Mortensgaard represents—both of these characters reflecting the disgust Ibsen felt for politicians, a disgust that led him in one of his notes to *The Wild Duck* to suggest that politicians and journalists might serve nicely for vivisection experiments. And there was the ineffectualness of Brendel, who with his visionary dreams and his lack of practical sense mirrored Ibsen's scorn of those who claimed to be poets in spirit, enjoying visions of great brilliance and yet nauseated, they said, by the thought of having to write it all down. Equally there is good reason to suppose that some of the more positive elements also grew out of this visit and out of the contacts he made or renewed: Carl Snoilsky, whose company he enjoyed for several days at Molde, seems to have served in some measure as the model for Rosmer; and Snoilsky's second wife provided something of Rebecca.

Above all, however, it was the pettiness and the self-seeking that he could not stomach, the air of narrow provinciality which to him seemed to characterize such a great deal of Norwegian public and private life. The speech that he delivered to a workers' meeting in Trondheim, only about a week after his arrival in the country, expressed both his impatience with democracy as it was then operating and his conviction that what was lacking was nobility of mind: 'Our democracy, as it now is [he said], is hardly in a position to deal with these problems. An element of nobility must find its way into our public life, into our government, among our representatives and into our press. Of course I am not thinking of nobility of birth nor of money, nor a nobility of learning, nor even of ability or talent. What I am thinking of is a nobility of character, of mind and of will.' These are sentiments one finds, in almost identical phrases, not only among his preliminary notes to *The Wild Duck*, but also allotted to Rosmer at that moment when he seeks to define his mission in life. Democracy is no better than the individuals who constitute it; and some form of *individual* regeneration is necessary if the ruthlessness of the party politician and the brutishness of the masses are to be vanquished.

This is one of the things Ibsen stressed when, on one of those rare occasions when he was persuaded to give an opinion about his own work, he offered an explanation of the meaning of *Rosmersholm*; in response to an inquiry from some grammar-school boys in Christiania, he agreed that the play dealt among other things with 'the need to work', but went on to draw attention to the conflict within the individual between principle and expediency, between conscience and acquisitiveness, between the 'progressive' and the 'conservative' in his nature, pointing out at the same time the difference in tempo in the way these things change. *Rosmersholm* considers the dialectics of change, and the consequences for the individuals concerned, that follow an encounter between a predominantly conservative nature and a predominantly progressive one: Rosmer, contemplative by nature, conservative by family, generous by inclination, of the highest personal integrity, and with his roots deep in a landed tradition; and Rebecca, swept along by her passions, of questionable antecedents, 'advanced' in her thinking, and with a ruthless will-power. He is stimulated by her example to act, to take personal decisions, to commit himself; and she is moved by his example to adopt some of the Rosmer scruples. Both of them have a vision of glory as the consummation of their endeavours, a glad cause, stimulating not strife but the friendly rivalry of noble minds, all splendid. But the reality of it is profound disappointment. Rebecca is 'ennobled', but in winning generosity of mind loses her power to act; Rosmer in daring to commit himself to action discovers that he has unwittingly but inevitably involved himself in guilt; and any joy they may separately have had from life is killed.

Between the policies of Rosmer and the earlier Gregers, the difference is fundamental: Gregers seeks to impose a general regulation, Rosmer wants rather to interpose *himself*, to make a personal contribution by mixing with his fellows and helping them to self-help—there is, he says, no other way. One of the reasons for his failure is that he is too fine-grained, too passively receptive, too retiring for the evangelical life. *Rosmersholm* is a refinery in which all the roughage is extracted from existence—is it not said that Rosmer children have never cried, nor the men ever laughed?—and in which all sense of initiative is filtered away. Rebecca testifies how it kills joy, and some of her remarks show how she suspects it kills sorrow, too; indeed, that it annihilates all the stronger, cruder, and more elemental aspects of life. The innocence of saintliness and the innocence of pathetic gullibility are equally Rosmer's, and he is greatly vulnerable; he has no idea how pitilessly he is manipulated by others, he sees very little of what really goes on. He stands there as one whose authority is largely inherited, taken from the family name; and also whose opinions are 'received', taken from the stronger personalities he yields to: first Brendel who was in the early days his tutor, then Kroll to whom he had turned for advice ever since his student days, and finally Rebecca. When ultimately his faith in Rebecca is destroyed, the ideals she has represented for him also crumble, their validity for him derives only from a faith in their guarantor, and it is characteristic of him that he turns at once to Kroll for a replacement of faith. When Brendel reappears to show himself a broken man, this betokens yet a further assault on what pass for Rosmer's convictions. His ideals, dependent as they are on the borrowed life they take from their sponsors, are not sturdy enough for independent existence, so that when at the end a final claim is made on Rosmer's faith—that Rebecca loves him—he is drawn as by an obsession to demand a living sacrifice, to request that the total personality should underwrite this new proposal.

But whereas Rosmer comes to rely utterly on this 'advanced' woman who has invaded his house, she herself, whose past has been a Nietzschean amoral life 'beyond good and evil' and who has all the instinctive ruthlessness of an animal of prey, fails victim to the insidious power of the Rosmer tradition. She encounters something, a sense of scruple, that turns out to be even stronger than her own pagan will, and she submits to it, numbed, 'ennobled'. The two things—integrity and initiative, innocence and committal, nobility of mind and tenacity of purpose, or however they are termed—seem on this evidence totally incompatible, mutually exclusive; and in this respect the play is profoundly pessimistic. The point where such destinies finally meet and merge is death; when, as Rosmer insists, the two of them become one, one course alone is adequate for *her* to prove her love, for *him* to prove his will, and for both to invite a just retribution for their guilty past.

It is this more than anything that invalidates the traditional question as to whether this play is a Rebecca tragedy or a Rosmer tragedy, for it is both and it is neither. The world that Ibsen constructs in *Rosmersholm* is a world of relationships, a lattice of conjoined characters linked each to each, in which dramatically speaking it is less important to evaluate the constituent elements as discrete phenomena than it is to see how they stand to each other; less important to see how they separately change than it is to see how, in the flux of changing circumstance, the relations between them change; less important to 'place' them by political belief, or psychological type, than it is to note the sightings they separately take on each other, and continue to take (often with unexpected results) in the light of new events; not forgetting that any change in these latticed relationships will be reflected in changes all round, in the sense that Rosmer's relations with Kroll, or Rebecca's, are also functions of their own private relationship, and that any change *there* will have its consequences *here*.

Consider, to take an extreme example, the strangely influential role of Beata, Rosmer's deceased wife, who 'exists' in the play not by reason of her physical presence but solely through the memories and through the assessments of those who remembered her. We know her only through them and what they say: Rosmer, though during her lifetime repelled by her overpassionate nature which he obviously associated with the growing insanity that drove her to suicide in the mill stream, can now think of her with tenderness; Rebecca, who at first speaks sympathetically of her until circumstances make her change her words; Kroll, whose sister she was and who puts first one and then a very different interpretation on some of her last actions; Mortensgaard, to whom she wrote a secret and compromising letter shortly before her death; and Mrs. Helseth, the housekeeper and intermediary between them. Such items constitute bearings, taken from vantage points that can be approximately determined because those who occupy them *appear* and so declare themselves. But of course there is no neat answer. Instead of all converging upon some single point of corroboration, their testimonies are so widely divergent that together they do no more than demarcate an area in which a number of different interpretations of Beata are possible. Allowances have to be made, corrections calculated—for individual bias, for distorted or defective vision, for deceit. How ignorant is Rosmer of the real state of affairs? How unscrupulous is Rebecca? How reliable Mortensgaard? Statements about Beata have not only a demonstrative but also a betrayal value; they are also *admissions*, sometimes involuntary, which provide a two-way link with every other character in the drama, except possibly Brendel. Any change in the relationships among those who make these admissions tends to be reflected there, as well as in their attitude to each other.

Further variables can add to the complexity of the dramatic structure. When, for example, Ulrik Brendel is announced, and before he shows himself, the three people assembled in the living-room line up their minds on this new phenomenon: for Kroll, it is that 'waster' whom he last heard of as being in the workhouse; for Rebecca, it is that 'strange man' of whom she wonders that he is still alive; and for Rosmer—to the astonishment of both Kroll and the housekeeper who cannot think that Brendel is a fit person for the living-room at Rosmersholm—he is, as a former tutor in the house, welcome. Three snap bearings help to locate this as yet unknown quantity. *After* he has made his appearance, and after it has been noted not only what valuation he places on himself but also what by his conduct he involuntarily reveals, the initial bearings can be given some adjustment and thus one's ideas about those who took them refined. The importance of looking to the relations, expressed and implied, *between* the characters and not merely to the characters as independent creations is underlined by the letter Ibsen wrote on 25 March 1887 to Sofie Reimers. Invited to play Rebecca in the first Kristiania production, she had begged Ibsen's advice; his answer was that she would do well to note carefully what the other characters said about Rebecca, and not make the mistake of studying the part in isolation. Expanding this, one might say that the truth about the individual characters lies within an area bounded by: what they assert is the case; what they wantonly or unwittingly conceal; what they betray of themselves; and what they draw by way of comment from others. And when it is remembered that it is quite possible for these characters to mislead, to be misled or misinformed, or to be in the grip of instincts or impulses they cannot wholly comprehend, then the unreliability of the raw, untreated evidence is at once apparent. To fit in the separate parts as coherent items in a shifting pattern of event and belief is very largely a question of allotting appropriate values to the various hints, suggestions, and allusions the play is strewn with. What hidden meanings in the opening conversation between Rebecca and Kroll, for example, are subsequently brought to light by the momentary revelation that he had once been infatuated by her? What modifications must be made to Rosmer's implicit allegation that Beata was over-sexed, when his attitude to Rebecca, and the evidence of the past year of their living alone together in the house, carries the suggestion that he himself was under-sexed? And with such suspicions, should one then begin to wonder where in fact the sterility in his marriage to Beata lay—with her, as she was given to understand, or with him? How much had Kroll suspected about Rebecca before, that his thrust about her one-time relations with Dr. West struck home? And by implanting the idea that she had been guilty of incest, was he merely taking revenge on her with the same weapon she had already employed on his sister Beata: fostering suspicion on a minimum of evidence, knowing just how vulnerable her mind was to such suggestions? All these are things that cause one to look again at remarks that are otherwise deceptively obvious or perversely obscure.

* * *

Truth, its establishment and its promotion, is a thing all three plays have something to say about. In *An Enemy of the People* truth is provable and demonstrable; it inhabits a few scribbled lines of an analyst's report, it is expressible as a chemical formula. Stockmann, in becoming its spokesman, provokes a bold pattern of communal response to the revelations which, by the authority of science, he is able to make; and the local community is goaded into disposing itself in attitudes of hostility round the main character. Truth lights up the whole as from a central pendant fitting, a naked lamp lowered into the dark places of society, making a composition in strong light and shade. Each individual is the incarnation of the principles he professes, or lack of them; attitudes are adopted and persisted in, word and deed are concerted, and there is plain speaking. In *Rosmersholm* on the other hand, truth is an equivocal thing, being no more than what anybody at any particular time believes to be the case; it is a matter of partly knowing, or not knowing any better; there is no real laying bare of fact but rather a submission of possibilities, no establishment of what in reality was so, but an appeal to plausibility; any authenticity can be substantiated only by stealthy and oblique methods. Things are as they seem, or as they can be made to seem, and genuine motives are buried beneath layer upon layer of self-deception and duplicity; secret shifts and subsidences are for ever taking place in the minds of those concerned, and lighting is dim and indirect and full of flickering cross-shadows, and the wool is pulled over more than one pair of eyes.

The path leading from the earlier drama to the later runs from the outspoken to the unspoken, from bluff honesty to shifty evasiveness, from the self-evident to the merely ostensible, from proclamation to dissimulation, from the ingenuous to the disingenuous, from open debate and public uproar to secret eavesdropping and private intimation, from events urged on by a live issue to events brought up short by a dead woman. By the polluted baths there is enacted a tableau, a positioning of one to many in a generally radial pattern of static relationships, with Stockmann as the hub and cynosure. Beside the millstream, on the other hand, none of the characters is central in the same way, and instead of the build-up of a linear pattern one finds a sequence of positional changes, a ballet of death in which the manoeuvres of the principals trace out a complex pattern of movement. In *An Enemy of the People* the author fashioned a vessel, a parabolic mould, into which he poured his wrath. *Rosmersholm*, however, has no such containing walls; its parts hold together rather on the analogy of particles in a complex magnetic field, they cohere not in obedience to some central solar force but rather because the resultant of all the various and varying attractions and repulsions they exert (or have exerted upon them) moves them the way it does. There is nothing at the centre except Nothing, the great void to which Brendel is finally attracted, and which draws the two anguished principals as though into the eye of a vortex. By comparison with *An Enemy of the People*, *Rosmersholm* seems to dispose over an extra dimension, and to enjoy a dynamic rather than a static existence; it differs from the earlier drama as a mobile differs from a blue-print, the one making a seemingly arbitrary but actually carefully balanced and *necessary* pattern of movement, and the other displaying all the clarity and self-assurance of something that recognizes its own dimensional limitations. By these tokens *The Wild Duck* is photographic, rather, and so ordered as to give an astonishingly successful illusion of perspective depth.

Hand in hand with these changes went an extra care in what Ibsen termed the 'individualization' of character and other 'finesses' attaching to the creation of dramatic dialogue. So, for instance, in conversation with John Paulsen some time in the early 1880s about 'the thousand and one finesses of dramatic art', he is reported to have asked whether his companion had ever considered 'how the dialogue in a play ought to have a different timbre if it was meant to be spoken in the morning from what it would be at night'. In letters written whilst engaged on revising *The Wild Duck*, he stressed that his attention was being given to the 'energetic individualization of character' and the finer formulation of the dialogue; and many years later, when replying to a young Frenchman who wanted permission to translate this play, he returned to this matter and pointed out the great demands the play makes on any translator, since 'one must be extremely familiar with the Norwegian language to be able to understand how thoroughly each separate character in the play has his own individual and idiosyncratic mode of expression'. Ibsen had always been an extremely conscientious artist, painstaking in the care that he gave the successive drafts of his work; now, and especially from *The Wild Duck* onward, he applied his massive revisionary capacity to the problem of the finer delineation of character; the separate figures are now no longer in the first instance the embodiment of general principles or attitudes, but instead personalities whose individuality and uniqueness are emphasized at every point in the drama. They cease to be object lessons, and become instead subjects of study. It is one of the chief fascinations of the draft manuscripts of these plays that they document at a number of points this process of 'individualization'.

Of the *fact* of some fundamental change in Ibsen's writing about the time of these three plays, there is general recognition, although there is not the same unanimity about where precisely to locate the turning point, nor how best to style it. Some critics have seen it as a transition from the 'social' to the 'visionary', from the 'naturalistic' to the 'symbolic', from the 'problematical' to the 'psychological'; there have been arguments in favour of calling the earlier group 'moralist' and for distinguishing *two* later phases, the 'humanist' and the 'visionary'; whilst yet another critic has argued persuasively for regarding the shift as being from a 'demonstrative' to an 'evocative' mood. It may indeed be necessary to relate the change to terms even more fundamental than these, and to see the crux as being a substantial shift in Ibsen's whole scheme of values. Writing to Theodor Caspari on 27 June 1884, Ibsen confessed that he had long since given up making general or universal demands, believing that one could not with any real justification make such blanket claims on people, and added: 'I do not believe any of us can do anything other or anything better than realize ourselves in truth and in spirit.' What seemed to matter to him now were particulars rather than generalities; his attention was addressed to private dilemma rather than public abuse, to what was individual and personal rather than typical or representative. He abandoned collective indictment for singular, distinctive investigation; he became less comprehensive in his scrutiny of things, more selective, more penetrative; and with it all went an increasing impatience with the mass mind and all its works.

INGA-STINA EWBANK

Shakespeare, Ibsen, and Rome:
A Study in Cultural Transmission

When, in the winter of 1848–49, Henrik Ibsen wrote his first play—*Catiline: A Drama in Three Acts*—he had small Latin and less English. And yet what he produced—only to discover that no theater wanted to produce it—could well have been described as having been begotten upon Sallust by Shakespeare.[1]

When, twenty-five years later, Ibsen published the work that he was always to regard as his magnum opus—the two-part, or ten-act, "world-historical drama" of *Emperor and Galilean* (1873)—he was far more deeply read in Latin sources but had still not acquired English (nor was he ever to do so), and he was now anxious not to be seen in the context of a Shakespearean tradition. To Edmund Gosse, who had criticized him for not writing *Emperor and Galilean* in verse and "not support[ing] the heroic dignity of the principal character," Ibsen replied: "My new play is no tragedy in the old style" and "We no longer live in Shakespeare's time."[2]

These two Roman plays—one set in the dying days of the republic, the other in the late empire—are the only Ibsen plays not set in Norway, whether past, as in his earlier plays, or present, as in the plays by which the world's theaters now mainly know him. They make a convenient pair of touchstones for the transmission of Shakespeare.

From *Shakespeare and Cultural Traditions: The Selected Proceedings of the International Shakespeare Association World Congress, Tokyo, 1991,* edited by Tetsuo Kishi, Roger Pringle, and Stanley Wells, pp. 229–42. Published by University of Delaware Press. Copyright © 1994 by Associated University Presses.

It would be easy—and partially true—to say that the two plays are antithetically opposed in their relation to Shakespeare. To say, that is, that in *Catiline* Ibsen—a twenty-year-old apothecary's apprentice, writing in the cultural backwater of a small Norwegian town—accepts Shakespeare, at third hand, as a dramatic and cultural model; and that in *Emperor and Galilean*—as a middle-aged citizen of Europe (after nine years of exile in Italy and Germany) and an established writer with a strong sense of the mission to create a drama that would embody and speak to his own age—he rejects that model at first hand. The acceptance was at third hand, insofar as Scandinavia received Shakespeare transmuted through the great romantic German translators, critics, and dramatists.[3] As late as the 1870s the Danish critic Georg Brandes could claim that Shakespeare had been "re-born" in August Wilhelm Schlegel.[4] If, in nineteenth-century England, Shakespeare came to stand for national culture, in northern Europe he came, via German culture, to stand for the essence of romanticism. In Ibsen's own language, the romantic poet-dramatist Oehlenschläger had held that Shakespeare was "the colossus who should be the model for every modern dramatist."[5] To mature Ibsen, this "Shakespeare" had become one of the ubiquitous ghosts that Mrs. Alving finds between the lines of whatever she reads: "all sorts of old dead opinions and beliefs."[6]

It is not surprising, then, that traditionally[7] Shakespeare has been seen as the crutch on which Ibsen leaned when he wrote his early and historical plays but which he had to throw away so that, for example, the "modern tragedy" about a woman in a man's society that he wrote in Amalfi in 1879 would become *A Doll's House* and not a blank verse play about a duchess.

But I said that all this is a partial truth, and my argument in this paper is that Ibsen's two Roman plays do not simply represent, respectively, acceptance and rejection of Shakespeare: that the latter is in some important ways more Shakespearean than the former; and that the contrast between them, in terms of Shakespearean transmission, is that between an externally imposed form on the one hand, and an intuitively absorbed and transmuted form on the other. And by using the word *form* here, I do not intend to be "formalist" but to imply elements of aesthetics, ethics, and politics, all rolled into one cultural form.

That Ibsen came to begin his dramatic career with Roman history was partly a matter of availability. In the hope of escaping from the Grimstad apothecary's shop, he was studying, in his spare moments, for the *artium*—the examination that would enable him to matriculate as a university student—and among his Latin set texts were the historical monographer Gaius Sallustius Crispus's *Bellum Catilinae* as well as Cicero's speeches against Catiline. Ibsen's endnote to the first edition of the play (1850) assumes the same background reading in his own readers (who were in fact very few: only 45 copies sold in the first year) and is defiantly unapologetic about the way he has used history:

> The factual background of this present drama is too familiar for it not to be immediately obvious how far it differs from historical truth; and also that history has only been utilized to a limited extent, so that it must be considered primarily as a vehicle for the underlying idea of the play.[8]

This "underlying idea" was to be defined for the reader in the preface Ibsen wrote to the revised edition of the play that he published in 1875. He points out that *Catiline* adumbrates much of what his later writings have been about: "the clash of ability and aspirations, of will and possibility."[9]

Indeed, the idea does not so much underlie as overlay the historical action, from the first lines of Catiline's opening soliloquy:

> I must! I must! In my soul's depths
> A voice commands, and I *will* follow it;—
> I feel the strength and courage for something better,
> For something higher than this life—
> This endless round of dissipated pleasures![10]

Sallust wrote of the conspiracy of Catiline because it was of exemplary importance, epitomizing all that was wrong at the end of an epoch of Roman history.[11] Ibsen wrote of Catiline because he found him a compelling individual—who happened to have lived in Rome. Unlike Ben Jonson's *Catiline* (which will be more familiar to students of Shakespeare and which Ibsen did of course not know), Ibsen's play is not about a corrupt power struggle in a corrupt state, but about a man driven to rebellion and defeat by an ambition that he himself likens to Icarus's (act 2; *SV* 1:81). As against Jonson's meticulous classicism and anatomy of political morality in the pre-Caesarian era of the republic, Ibsen's *Catiline* is set in a kind of historical/geographical/political vacuum: we never see the opposition to Catiline, except through his eyes and in his words; there is no Senate, no Caesar (so shadily involved in Jonson's play, though exonerated by Sallust), no Cicero. Compared to the satirical expositions of moral turpitude in Jonson's *Catiline*, the "endless round of dissipated pleasures" referred to in Ibsen's opening lines is very delicately dramatized: a few young men with wine leaves in their hair, drinking and singing, suggesting little more dissipation than Osvald does when he describes, in *Ghosts*, how the artists live in Paris.

Leonard Digges records (allowing for poetic license) how audiences were "ravish'd" by Shakespeare's *Julius Caesar*:

> When some new day they would not brooke a line
> Of tedious (though well laboured) *Catiline*.[12]

But to a generation of scholars alerted to the significance of tragedies of state, the contrast between those two plays is less clearcut[13] and the excitement (such as it is) in Jonson's *Catiline* rests exactly in the "well laboured" effect of always hearing the voice of Rome, whether in caricature, as when Curius goes off to bed Fulvia (a favor bought with the betrayal of Catiline) on a couplet,

> Rome will be sack'd, her wealth will be our prize;
> By public ruin, private spirits must rise;
>   (2.1.361–62)[14]

or as a moving realization of the political morass through which the Chorus confusedly stumbles at the end of act 4—

> Now do our ears before our eyes
>   Like men in mists
> Discover who'd the state surprise,
>   And who resists?
>   (4.7.20–23)

—to be answered, at the opening of act 5, by Petreius's speech to the soldiers, pleading with them to fight for the republic, in a rhetoric that embodies all its ideals:

> For the rais'd temples of th'immortal gods,
> For all your fortunes, altars, and your fires,
> For the dear souls of your lov'd wives and children,
> Your parents' tombs, your rites, laws, liberty,
> And, briefly, for the safety of the world.
>   (4.1.15–19)

This political and theatrical vision of Rome is beyond young Ibsen's reach. "Rome" exists in his play only in the mind of the self-absorbed hero. In the present it is an obstacle to his self-realization:

They look down on me, despise me, those wretches—
They do not know how fast my heart beats
For justice and liberty and for every cause
Which nobly stirred in any human breast!
(Act 1; *SV* 1:51)

And Rome of the past is an ideal to which he claims to aspire:

The time when every Roman gladly gave his life
For the honour of his fatherland,
And sacrificed all,—to save its glory!
(Act 2: *SV* 1.79)

As in these lines, there are sentiments of traditional *Romanitas* in the hero's proclamations, but they remain vague and unsubstantiated, for this Catiline is not a political animal. The conflict that destroys him is embodied in his response to two women: the affection for his wife, Aurelia (a sentimentalized version of Brutus's Portia), and the passion for Furia, the source's Fulvia translated into a vestal virgin seeking to revenge her dead sister's seducer (or Catiline). Aurelia nearly persuades Catiline to abandon Rome for a life with her in a pastoral retreat, a regained paradise where, she tells him, "You will dig the ground, and I shall plant the flowers" (act 2; *SV* 1:68). Furia's ambivalent love-hatred inflames his ambition to rise up and conquer Rome. (The sexual psychology and politics of this response is another paper.) The action is structured on this quite unhistorical triangle—the germ of the two-women pattern that runs through so many later Ibsen plays. In the last act Catiline loses all his supporters in a horrendous offstage battle; he comes on stage, devastated, and is prevailed upon, by Furia, to cut the last bond that binds him to humanity by stabbing Aurelia to death (offstage). He then makes Furia stab *him*, thus fulfilling the prophecy spoken earlier by the Ghost of Sulla:

Thou shalt fall by thine own hand,
Yet shall another strike thee down.
(Act 3; *SV* 1:96)

But before he has time to expire, Aurelia—ever forgiving and not quite dead—staggers on; and husband and wife die, reconciled and comforted, in each other's arms—or, rather as the stage direction has it, with "Catiline's *head sinking down on to* Aurelia's *breast*"—in an assertion, much like the end of *Peer Gynt*, of the power of love and *das ewig weibliche*:

> You have conquered the powers of darkness with your love.
>   (Act 3; *SV* 1:114)

Because this play is so far from being a masterpiece, the strands of cultural tradition are so clearly discernible, lying there side by side rather than interwoven. In his preface to the 1875 edition of *Catiline* Ibsen tells us to read it as an image both of the poet and of his time. He did not reprint the note that declared lack of interest in Roman history as such. Instead the preface claims that he had consciously provided an alternative reading to Sallust's and Cicero's, feeling that few historical personages "have been more exclusively in the [interpretative] power of their opponents than has Catiline."[15] The pressures that generated that reading and the play were, he claims, both personal and public. Catiline, the misunderstood Roman, became the figure of Henrik Ibsen in Grimstad, where

> while great things were happening in the stormy world outside, I found myself at war with the small community where I was desperately cramped by my own position and circumstances. (*SV* 1:120)

The "great things" were, of course, the political events of 1848:

> It was a time of upheavals. The February Revolution, the uprisings in Hungary and elsewhere, the war over Schleswig. (*SV* 1:119)

Though Ibsen did not know it, the 1848 revolutions did form the pretext of a number of *Catiline* plays. Alexandre Dumas, with Maquet, cashed in on the February revolution almost immediately with an intrigue play about the Roman rebel; and, more relevantly, in 1851 Ferdinand Kürnberger published a play in Frankfurt that completes the transformation of Catiline into a freedom hero. Hermann Speck calls it *"ein Trauendenkmal am Grabe der Revolution."*[16]

To us, who have learned to distrust authors in their prefaces (if we have not deconstructed their existence altogether), *Catiline* hardly suggests that Ibsen had been able to read the present through the past. He had written ardent poems on each of the causes he lists in the preface, but what the play achieves is an uneasy marriage of Byronic self-dramatization with an attempt to set up an isolated deed in Roman history as an analogue of the present. But this is not how it struck some of his own contemporaries. The first review to appear began by welcoming the play and its author because of "a certain Shakespearean strength and seriousness." And, it went on, even the reader who only looks for what is relevant will find "in *Catiline*, just as much as in Shakespeare's *Coriolanus*, a moment which is forever recurring in the life of nations" and that will recur "until the republicans, on the last day of tyranny, can sing their victory hymns on the grave of the last despot."[17] Through the rhetoric of this young Norwegian student-reviewer "Shakespeare" emerges as a cultural construct: a code for "strength," "seriousness" and for timeless opposition to tyranny and repression.

At this point Ibsen had read little Shakespeare and seen none. What he had read would have been in Danish translation, and the handling of certain situations in *Catiline* suggests particular acquaintance with *Macbeth* (for example, Furia taunts Catiline with not having "a woman's courage"[18] and the manner of his death is foretold by an equivocating apparition). But it is clearly *Julius Caesar* that has acted as a catalyst for Ibsen; that is, if we assume that he understood Shakespeare's play not as an exploration of the necessary events of Roman history but as a play exclusively about Brutus (to whom, of course, Catiline was a near forerunner). This is the Brutus whose tragedy, according to A. W. Schlegel, was that

> from the purity of his mind and his conscientious love of justice [he was] unfit to be the head of a party in a state entirely corrupt.[19]

Ibsen's Catiline has to be seen in a tradition in which Brutus is read as being closely related to Hamlet and in which both are seen, in the words of Brandes, as "profound dreamers and high-minded idealists." The matter of Rome is assumed to be of secondary importance. "Everywhere in *Julius Caesar* we feel the proximity of *Hamlet*" is how Brandes concludes the second chapter on *Julius Caesar* in his monumental book on Shakespeare, having devoted the first to the "fundamental defect" of the play: the failure of Shakespeare, "in whose eyes the old republics shone transfigured," to appreciate the greatness of Caesar.[20] As late as 1908, in his essay on *Julius Caesar*, August Strindberg works from the same critical stance when he reproaches Shakespeare for not giving the play its proper historical perspective. He ought to have reminded the audience that Octavius Caesar is to become the Augustus of *pax romana*. Had he done so—and then Strindberg starts describing the play that he thinks Shakespeare should have written and that much twentieth-century criticism thinks he did write—

> then the drama would have had an infinite perspective, no beginning, no end, something of world-historical endlessness where the

actors come and go but the theater remains, where the audience is always new, but the play is the same, its action showing how

> Imperious Caesar, dead and turn'd to clay
> Might stop a hole to keep the wind away.

Pompei, Caesar, Brutus, Antony, Augustus—it's a series where each term is like the square root of the one before.[21]

Strindberg is typically explicit about assumptions that were implicit in the tradition of a nineteenth-century Scandinavian "Shakespeare" where the Roman plays were perceived as a matter of great individuals, not of historical drama—of inter- and intrapersonal, not political, conflicts. We must not blame the German critics for this.[22] Schlegel, lecturing on *Julius Caesar*, already had emphasized how "the public life of ancient Rome is called up from its grave and exhibited before our eyes";[23] and later in the century Ulrici wrote on the plays' historical and political vision of Rome moving inevitably from a republican to a monarchical form of government, and of this movement necessitating an oligarchical transition period. Hence, according to Ulrici, Shakespeare shows us that both Caesar, aiming at monarchy, and Brutus, fighting to retain republicanism, were wrong because both represented "a thing of the past" and that Antony, identified with oligarchy, was right because he had "the immediate present" on his side.[24]

But Ibsen, in 1848, was untouched by such insights, and if his "Shakespeare" was third-hand, it was because it was instead mediated through German *Sturm und Drang* drama, notably Schiller's *The Robbers* (*Die Räuber*, 1780). If Brutus is a "profound dreamer and high-minded idealist" ineffectually rebelling against a corrupt society, so is Karl von Moor; and the German hero is also, like Catiline, capable of unspeakable atrocities even while we are invited to admire in him a personal heroism. Admittedly Sallust, otherwise so critical of Catiline, admires him in his death. He writes movingly of the battlefield covered in bodies, all lying where they had stood to fight, and all wounded on the front. And,

> Catiline was found far in advance of his men amid a heap of slain enemies, still breathing slightly, and showing in his face the indomitable spirit which had animated him when alive. (lxi)

Even Jonson's Cato allows Catiline

> A brave bad death.
> Had this been honest now, and for his country,

As 'twas against it, who had e'er fallen greater?
(5.9.84–86)

So, apart from that, he was the noblest Roman of them all. But the death of Ibsen's Catiline, as of Schiller's Karl von Moor, is not into *Romanitas* but into personal, self-defined virtue. Moor at the end kills his "angel," Amelia, as Catiline kills Aurelia; and in both plays female suffering and love are foregrounded so that we end with a confused picture of the hero as a kind of Byronic Brutus, much sinned against, deeply flawed (not least sexually), and greatly noble.

Ibsen's own unease with this "Shakespeare" is obvious. In the immediately following years he was to encounter a few Shakespeare plays on stage, in Copenhagen and Dresden.[25] In 1855 he was involved in a production of *As You Like It* at the Bergen theater where he was stage instructor, and the same year he gave a lecture, of which tantalizingly only the title survives, "William Shakespeare and His Influence on Scandinavian Art."[26] Whatever the lecture contained, by now he clearly felt that "influence" to be baneful. The 1850s and 1860s were for him a period of stock-taking vis à vis national culture and cultural consciousness, marked both by his own attempts at a national drama[27] and by a series of often combative articles. Thus, in 1861, writing on national versus popular theater in the Norwegian capital, Kristiania, he anatomizes the "Shakespeare" that has become a cultural status symbol. "In a society as under-developed as ours, the consciousness of being semi-educated produces a nightmarish fear of betraying one's lack of sophistication," and the result, he writes, is a conspiracy of pretense between critics and audiences who will

> applaud and admire a bad production of a so-called Shakespearean play, although they only partly understand it. But they have both read and been told that Shakespeare is a great author; sophisticated taste therefore demands that one likes him. That it is a perverse Shakespeare that is being offered, makes no difference, since they don't know the genuine one.[28]

How far, then, did Ibsen know "the genuine one"? He never confessed publicly to reading Shakespeare (or indeed to reading anything much, apart from the Bible), but in the later 1860s there are records of him borrowing Shakespeare texts from the Scandinavian library in Rome.[29] And Rome, of course, is the rub. Ibsen left Norway in 1864, not to return permanently for twenty-seven years. Unlike some other literary exiles—Conrad or Beckett—he remained monolingual, staying as a writer within his native language. At the same time the exile was, initially, a rejection of contemporary

Norwegian culture—politics, ethics, and aesthetics. He rejected a false nationalism that worshiped a Nordic past but left Denmark to fight Russia on its own. He did not want to return, he wrote from Rome in those early days, because he did not want his son to grow up among people whose aim was to be "Englishmen rather than human beings."[30] Englishness stood for a lax ("*slapp*") liberalism. And yet when he tried to define the society of artists and writers in Rome that he found so congenial, the only possible comparison was with "the atmosphere of Shakespeare's *As You Like It*."[31] In a sense he now developed a cultural tradition all his own, one which involved tremendous adjustments, not least vis à vis Shakespeare.

It was very soon after arriving in Rome that he conceived the idea of writing a play about Julian the Apostate, Roman Emperor from 361 to 363. The project came to occupy him for nearly nine years before it found its final form. Other plays kept intervening—*Brand* (1866), *Peer Gynt* (1867), and his first contemporary prose play, *The League of Youth* (1869). But to write *Emperor and Galilean* remained an obsession, an urge—as with Goethe's *Faust, Part II*, or George Eliot's *Romola*—to forge the consciousness of one's race on the anvil of world history. The result, like those two works, has been more revered than read, and—like so many Faustian offsprings—more read than performed. The experience of Italy prompted a return to Roman history: at Frascati he felt as if he "looked down upon the field where world history has fought its main battles."[32]

But the immediate impact of Rome had not been historical as much as aesthetic; the culture shock had released his own verbal and dramatic powers. Ibsen had brought to Rome the beginnings of an epic poem in iambic pentameters about a Kierkegaardian priest—a work that showed every sign of being stillborn until, in one epiphanic moment under the dome of St. Peter's, "a strong, clear form" for what he had to say came to him. Within three months he had written the play of *Brand*, in the rhyming tetrameters that are natural to Norwegian rhythms, even as they express the uncompromising nature of the hero. Although the landscape of *Brand* is the icy mountains and sunless fjords of Norway, the hero, like Christ in the Sistine Chapel, is "the new Adam," and his God is "young like Hercules." It was not classical art but the strength—even the sheer size—of the art of the High Renaissance and the baroque, of Michelangelo and Bernini, that had struck Ibsen. In *Brand* the energies of north and south meet in a huge vertical poem-play on the thrust of the human will to perfection. Rome had made Ibsen, but only to make him increasingly aware of the relativity of cultural traditions. "There is nothing eternal either about moral concepts or about the forms of art," he wrote to Brandes in 1871.[33]

Ibsen not only returned to reading Shakespeare in the period when the form of *Emperor and Galilean* slowly evolved, but he also received, as he was working on the final form of the play, a stimulus towards a new perception of Shakespeare as realistic, antiromantic. Brandes published his book *Critics and Portraits* in which the essay called "The Infinitely Small and the Infinitely Great in Poetry" praises Shakespeare's ability to make history "real" and to put the whole human being on stage. He discusses in particular two episodes in *1 Henry IV*—the talk of the Carriers in 2.1 and the spermaceti passage in 1.3— as evidence of Shakespeare's technique of injecting color, life, and texture through small and apparently irrelevant details. Ibsen made no comment on Brandes' Shakespearean criticism as such, but his overall response to the tenor of Brandes' lectures shows a quite untypical excitement: "A more dangerous book could never fall into the hands of a pregnant writer."[34]

The long pregnancy resulted in a work with more Shakespearean features than have been traditionally acknowledged. In *Catiline* the hero's will is torn between a fair beloved and a dark lady; Brand thinks that he—and he alone—is doing God's will until a voice out of the avalanche that kills him proclaims that "He is *deus caritatis*." Julian's will is projected, throughout the two parts of *Emperor and Galilean*, as a search for truth at once metaphysical, religious, and political. In this he commands admiration, like Shakespeare's Brutus; like Brutus he is tragic because his will to create a new order, a "Third Empire," clashes with historical necessity. Like the murder of Caesar, Julian's apostasy does not bring about a new and better order but a resurgence of the forces he has been combating. In part 1 of *Emperor and Galilean*, subtitled *Caesar's Apostasy*, we see the hero ascendant, against a background of Christianity in decadence and disarray; in part 2, *Emperor Julian*, we see him in slow decline against a resurgent Christianity, a structure that may indicate subliminal memories of *Antony and Cleopatra* (a play that has certainly left verbal traces in the 1875 revision of *Catiline*).

Emperor and Galilean is of course an enormously ambitious work, using Roman history to write about the present and about all history.[35] Ibsen never stopped claiming both contemporary and timeless "world-historical" relevance for this work—as in the speech in 1887 where he stated his belief that the present age is "a closure, and that from it something new is in the process of being born"; that "the scientific doctrine of evolution" operates in all elements of life so that human ideals are not eternally valid; and "that the ideals of our age, by suffering eclipse, show a trend towards what I have intimated in my drama *Emperor and Galilean* by the term "the Third Empire."[36] There are obvious connections with European philosophy, such as Schopenhauer's idea of a "world will" that Ibsen may have met through von Hartmann's *Philosophy of the Unconscious*, and Hegel's *Philosophy of History*.[37] And, though Ibsen did not know Nietzsche at this stage, his own exploration of Apollonian and Dionysiac powers was exactly contemporary with that which was published, in 1872, as *The Birth of Tragedy*.

But those connections have been much written about, and my concern here is with how a new apprehension of Shakespeare—without acknowledgment and possibly without Ibsen being all that conscious of it—helped Ibsen to make Roman history "real." On the purely stylistic level this may seem absurd: Ibsen was soon to claim, appealing again to the theory of evolution, that "a tragedy in iambic pentameter is already as rare a phenomenon as the dodo";[38] and in the letter where he reminded Gosse that "we no longer live in Shakespeare's time" he was emphatic about having used prose in *Emperor and Galilean* to produce "the illusion of reality."[39] Yet it is precisely in the striving for that illusion, in the sense of making Roman history felt and meaningful to a reader or an audience, that Shakespeare comes in.

As in *Catiline*, Ibsen concentrates in his second Roman play on the hero, but this time the hero is a Roman in history: private and public issues are inseparable, as are religious and political ones. G. K. Hunter has written on how "the Roman Empire whose shadow lies over the deaths of Brutus and Cassius is seen not only as a political necessity but as a Roman necessity"[40] and much the same can be said of the play of Julian. Ibsen has so identified his hero with a stage of Roman history that every action Julian takes casts a shadow into the world of politics and every thought and feeling of his inner life is intertwined with the political and religious life of Rome. As in Shakespeare's histories, "the illusion of reality" does not prevent, but rather demands, the ritualizing of some of the action. In part 2, for example, two singing processions meet in the market place of Antioch—one of Christian martyrs going to their deaths, the other of Apollo worshipers, led by Emperor Julian—and their songs antiphonally present the play's dialectic:

> *The Procession of Apollo.*
> Lovely our joy as the sun warmly glows!
> *The Procession of Prisoners.*
> Blissful our groans as the martyr-blood flows.[41]

And part 1 ends in a climactic scene in Vienna where the final stages both of Julian's apostasy and of his assumption of imperial power are counterpointed with the chanting of the Our Father in the church above the catacombs in whose mysterious depths Julian thinks he has found the truth:

> Emperor Julian *throws the door wide open, to reveal the brightly lit church. The priests are at the high altar . . .*
>
> *Emperor Julian.* Free, free! Mine is the kingdom!

One of his followers adds: "And the power and the glory!" Only to be contradicted by the Choir in the church:

> *Choir.* Thine is the kingdom and the power and the glory . . . *in saecula saeculorum*, amen!
> (*SV* 7:225)

To stage this one would need the resources of the Tokyo Globe or perhaps the cinema. But the effect is not just of a proto-*Ben Hur*, nor do Ibsen's efforts to provide a dense local texture (so diametrically opposed a technique to that in *Catiline*) merely create a kind of dramatized *Last Days of Pompeii*, for the "shadow" of a world in transition everywhere colors this texture and makes it part of the central questioning. As in *Macbeth*, there is overwhelming confusion and perplexity in *Emperor and Galilean*. Both in the ten years of uncertain Christianity covered by part 1 and in the two years as Emperor and Hellene in part 2, the hero is forever trying to read signs—omens, dreams, ghostly appearances. And to choose—Emperor or Galilean—is to commit oneself to false readings.

This also means that the death of Julian is not a simple and nostalgically regretted defeat of a world order, as in Swinburne's almost contemporary lament that

> Thou hast conquered, O pale Galilean; the world has
>   grown grey from Thy breath.

The strengths *and* weaknesses of both Christian and Hellenic civilizations have been dramatized: and Julian—like Brutus—dies because he misread the signs of history.

Perhaps the most Shakespearean contribution to making history "real" lies in Ibsen's insistence in this play that history means people, many people. Catiline lived in a vacuum, interacting with a few characters of whom the kindest thing we can say is that they are archetypal. Julian's world is thronged: Ibsen creates its ethos in scenes and episodes apparently irrelevant to the hero's rise or fall but crucial to the historical life of the play, and to reminding us what the affairs of emperors and priests look like when viewed from the outside or from below. There is, in part 1, the poor barbarian King Knodomar who does not know enough Latin (or Norwegian) and so gets executed by command of the Emperor Constantius because he has addressed Julian as "Keiser" (or "Emperor") when he should have said "Caesar." And there are, in part 2, the people to whom it hardly matters whether they worship Christ or Apollo, as long as they eat well.

If I am right in thinking that this attention in Ibsen's second Roman play to what Brandes called "the infinitely small" is transmitted from Shakespeare, then Shakespeare via Ibsen reaches literally into the here and now, anticipating not so much a "Third Empire" as the kind of small questions asked—as well, of course, as infinitely great ones—at the Tokyo World Congress on Cultural Traditions. At the beginning of act 3 in part 2 of *Emperor and Galilean* a group of courtiers, teachers, poets, and rhetoricians are gathered, discussing the culture that Julian is insisting on. "I can't stand this life any longer," says one. "Rising with the sun, having a cold bath, and then running and fencing till you're ready to drop." And another one replies: "But it's all very good for you." To which the first retorts: "Is it good for you to eat seaweed and raw fish?"

NOTES

1. Several other names—Schiller's, for one—could of course have been cited in a paternity suit.

2. All Ibsen texts in this paper are, unless otherwise indicated, cited and literally translated from *Hundrersutgaven: Henrik Ibsens Samlede Verker*, 21 vols., ed. Francis Bull, Halvdan Koht, and Didrik Arup Seip (Oslo: Gyldendal, 1928–57), hereafter referred to as *SV*. The letter to Gosse is dated 15 January 1874: *SV* 17:121–23.

3. I do not mean to imply that all Scandinavian translators worked from German Shakespeare translations, though some did; and most were almost inevitably influenced by German Shakespeare criticism. "Third hand" refers to the further transmutation of Shakespeare through German *Sturm and Drang* drama.

4. According to Brandes, "it is as if in the middle of the eighteenth century—at the side of Goethe and Schiller—Shakespeare too had been born in Germany. He was born in 1564 in England; he was re-born in 1767 in his German translator. In 1597 *Romeo and Juliet* was published in London; in 1797 this tragedy was published in Berlin as a newly-born work" (*Hovedstrømninger i det nittende Aarhundredes Litteratur*, 6 vols. [1872–90; reprint, Copenhagen: Gyldendal, 1966], 2:56–57).

5. Cited from P. M. Mitchell, *A History of Danish Literature* (Copenhagen: Gyldendal, 1957), 112.

6. *Ghosts* (*Gengangere*), act 2.

7. See, e.g. Sverre Arestad, "Ibsen and Shakespeare: A Study in Influence," *Scandinavian Studies* 19 (1946): 89–104.

8. Cited from James Walter McFarlane's translation in *The Oxford Ibsen* 8 vols. (London: Oxford University Press, 1960–77), 1:108 which makes elegant sense of the somewhat clumsy prose in the original.

9. *SV* 1:101.

10. Literally translated from the 1850 text (*SV* 1:43). There are quite major verbal revisions in the 1875 version, the differences between the two texts approaching, if not equaling, those between the Q and F texts of *King Lear*.

11. Having resolved to write a history of the Roman people (which in fact he does by his digressions around the alleged main topic), he chose the conspiracy of Catiline, "*nam id facinus in primis ego memorabile existumo sceleris atque periculi novitate*" (for I regard that event as worthy of special notice because of the extraordinary

nature of the crime and the danger arising from it). Cited from *Sallust*, with an English Translation by J. C. Rolfe, Loeb Classical Library (1922, reprint, Cambridge: Harvard University Press, 1988). 4:4–5.

12. Quoted from Georg Brandes, *William Shakespeare* (London: Heinemann, 1898), 302.

13. In a brilliant essay G. K. Hunter demonstrated that Shakespeare was as much of a Roman historian as Jonson: "Both see the same central issue in Roman history. . . . For both of them the romance of *Romanitas* attaches to the traditional values of *fides, disciplina, pudicitia, libertas*—and for both of them these values are 'placed' inside the minds of unsuccessful individuals hypnotized by the past and incompetent to change the future" ("A Roman Thought: Renaissance Attitudes to History Exemplified in Shakespeare and Jonson," in *An English Miscellany*, ed. B. S. Lee [London: Oxford University Press, 1977], 114–15).

14. Quotations from Ben Jonson's *Catiline* are from the edition by W. F. Bolton and Jane F. Gardner (London: Edward Arnold, 1972).

15. Classical scholars have argued about the extent to which Sallust's *Catiline* was written as a defense of Caesar. Theories of the work's propagandist purpose are inextricably tied up with the question of the exact date of composition during a fateful few years: was it immediately after the Ides of March, or later, even as late as 40 B.C.? See Ronald Syme, *Sallust* (Berkeley and Los Angeles: University of California Press, 1964), chap. 9, "Sallust's Purpose."

16. "A funeral monument on the tomb of the revolution." Hermann B. G. Speck, *Katilina im Drama der Weltliteratur: Ein Beitrag zu vergleichender Stoffgeschichte des Römerdramas* (Leipzig: Max Hesse, 1906), 65.

17. Paul Botten Hansen, in the review that appeared in *Samfundsbladet*, a handwritten Kristiania (Oslo) students' magazine, on 13 April 1850, the day after the publication of *Catiline*. Quoted from the reprint in Karl Haugholt, "Samtidens Kritikk av Ibsens 'Catilina,'" *Edda* 52 (1952): 77.

18. The *Macbeth* echo is clearer still in the 1875 text, where Furia's challenge reads, "Are you a man,—and have not the courage of a woman?" (*SV* 1:156).

19. August Wilhelm Schlegel, *Dramatic Literature: Lectures*, trans. J. Black (London, 1815), 240.

20. Brandes, *William Shakespeare*, 304, 324, 306. Published originally in Danish (Copenhagen: Gyldendal, 1895–96), the work was translated partly by William Archer and partly by Diana White, both assisted by Mary Morison, but Brandes himself revised the proofs.

21. August Strindberg, "*Julius Caesar*: Shakespeare's Historical Drama" (the third of his *Letters to the Intimate Theatre*, 1908), in *Samlade Skrifter*, ed. John Landquist, 55 vols. (Stockholm: Albert Bonnier, 1912–1920), 50:119.

22. Werner Habicht, in his paper "Romanticism, Antiromanticism, and the German Shakespeare Tradition" . . . splendidly illustrates the range of German nineteenth-century attitudes to Shakespeare.

23. Schlegel, *Dramatic Literature*, 209.

24. H. Ulrici, *Shakespeare's Dramatic Art*, trans. L. D. Schmitz (London, 1876), 195ff.

25. On a study tour in 1852 he saw *Hamlet* and probably also *King Lear, Romeo and Juliet*, and *As You Like It* in Copenhagen, and again *Hamlet* as well as *Richard III* and *A Midsummer Night's Dream* in Dresden.

26. See *SV* 15:12.

27. Such as *The Burial Mound* (1850), *Lady Inger of Østråt* (1855), *The Feast at Solhaug* (1856), *The Vikings at Helgeland* (1858), and *Pretenders* (1863).

28. "De To Theatre i Christiania" (21 May 1861), in *SV* 15:255.

29. See Øyvind Anker, "Ibsen og Den skandinaviske Forening i Roma," *Edda* 56 (1956): 177.

30. Ibsen to Magdalene Thoresen, 3 December 1865 (*SV* 16:119).

31. Ibsen to Peter Hansen, 28 October 1980 (*SV* 16:318).

32. Ibsen to Paul Botten Hansen, 22 July 1866 (*SV* 16:160).

33. Ibsen to Georg Brandes, 17 February 1871 (*SV* 16:350).

34. Ibid., 4 April 1872 (*SV* 17:31).

35. An excellent introduction to the ambitions and achievements of this work, and in particular to its Hegelian bearings, is in Brian Johnston, *To the Third Empire: Ibsen's Early Drama* (Minneapolis: University of Minnesota Press, 1980), 224–71.

36. *SV* 15:410–11. Cited from McFarlane's translation, *Oxford Ibsen*, 4:608.

37. See, e.g., Edvard Beyer, *Ibsen: The Man and His Work* (London: Souvenir Press, 1978), 93–108.

38. Ibsen to Lucie Wolf, 25 May 1883 (*SV* 17:511).

39. Ibsen to Edmund Gosse, 15 January 1874 (*SV* 17:121–23).

40. Hunter, "A Roman Thought," 107.

41. Cited in McFarlane's translation, *Oxford Ibsen* 4:368.

ERIC BENTLEY

What Ibsen Has Meant

How does one get to know Ibsen? There are two ways: you read him or you see him performed.

He has had devoted readers. Those who have written books and essays about him have read him in two ways. First, they have delved into every sentence and every word, asking questions as they went along, pausing thoughtfully over every surprising noun, vivid verb, or nuanced adjective. Or, secondly, they have interrupted their reading to fill in the background, perusing authors Ibsen is known to have read or philosophers he may have been influenced by. From such intrinsic and extrinsic factors a new view of Ibsen tends to emerge: he should not be viewed as *this* kind of playwright but as *that*. His plays do not say what grandpa said they did, but what the latest arrival on the scholarly scene says they say.

I am describing the bulk of the critical literature on Ibsen as written by his readers. Spectators are represented only by theatre reviewers, whose feuilletons are not expected to go as deep or spread as broad. But could it be—this is the question I am about to raise—that the scholars are missing something—something essential—which intelligent theatre viewers and *re*viewers do not miss?

A play performed is subject to dictates of duration. Shakespeare called it a "two-hours traffic." Seeing a performance, one cannot stop over a passage

From *Southwest Review* 88, no. 4 (2003): 531–38. Copyright © 2003 by Eric Bentley.

and re-read it. One cannot put down the script and resume reading in the morning. There are dictates, too, of tempo and rhythm. One can silently read at any speed one chooses, with any crescendos and diminuendos. Whether rhythm is achieved depends on the reader. A performed play, on the other hand, is music, not written out, but sung and played. It may be several movements but it is one symphony and the short pauses between movements do not break the continuity, they neither block any build-up nor hinder any dénouement. The performance delivers a single experience both spiritual and emotional, with an immediate beginning, middle, and end. No critical account manages to define this experience. No critical account is the equivalent of it.

I am touching here on the old dispute: literature versus theatre. My own answer to that question has always been that a great play has two lives, both of them complete in their own way, a reading life in the study, a viewing life in the theatre. Shakespeare's plays lead both these lives happily. Byron's plays, on the other hand, are, for the most part, happier in the study, closer, let's say, to Milton than to Shakespeare. "Closet drama" is a mean-spirited name for work of this sort. What needs to be kept in mind is that the great closet dramas are set, like movies, in natural surroundings, whereas theatrical dramas are artificially set—in a wooden O or a baroque toy stage. One question to ask of the poet travelling in these realms is whether he *needs* the theatre—if he needs an audience—an audience being not just one spectator and another but a group that responds as a group. Theatre's impact is immediate. As spectator-auditor you take it in perforce as soon as it is spoken or mimed. You react together with your companions, you do so at once, and when it is over you don't feel it has been summed up or even perhaps totally clarified. You feel, shall we say? such emotions as you might feel at the end of a string quartet or a symphony. Elation perhaps. Joy. Or a deep, searing sadness. Or a strong negative response, like: "My God, the bottom has dropped out of the universe!" Or: "There *is* no God."

Did Ibsen need the theatre? His poetry and his verse plays certainly prove he could have got along quite nicely without it. And when he moved from so-called romantic verse to so-called realistic prose, under the influence of Georg Brandes, he could have written novels. He chose theatre. And he chose theatre not in its highbrow forms, but in the vein of what we call commercial theatre he took up the French well-made play.

I conclude then that he needed theatre. I also conclude that he needed the well-made play, not because it was commercial, but because it is well made. The well-made play had several characteristics that may have appealed to him, but one of them eclipses all the others in importance: it often presented *secrets revealed at climactic moments to explosive effect*. Whether it be the roof falling in or the floor dropping out, a bomb is thrown. (The possibility that the world itself would be blown up, which became real in the twentieth century, is latent in the work of Ibsen.) To change the metaphor a little, Ibsen can be seen as planting time-bombs, which, as they go off, mark the climaxes of a dramatic Action.

What is theatre? For one thing, it is a place where actors convert characters into roles. In Pirandello's *Six Characters In Search of An Author*, characters come on stage. For the reader in the study they are phantoms, creatures of the imagination. On stage, however, they are roles for actors who are present and are flesh and blood. Here Pirandello was making two rather complex points: 1. The actor who merely pretends to be someone is flesh and blood while the someone he pretends to be is not. 2. A character in theatre is not directly seen; what is seen is an actor pretending to be a character. And I make a mistake in calling these propositions mere points. They are factors in that form of communion and communication which we call theatre.

Who needs it? Ibsen, I'd say, didn't need it when he wrote *Brand* but he did need it when he presented to the world people such as Nora Helmer and Hedda Gabler, Halvard Solness and John Gabriel Borkman because these—and their brothers and sisters—needed to be roles as well as characters. Technically, what this means is that the playwright offers the actor opportunities to transform characters into roles. Hamlet is the greatest Shakespearean role because of what it gives the great actor on a silver platter: the opportunity to translate the idea of the character into visible, audible action that reaches out to an audience. Prospero is as great a character but not as great a role because it offers the actor only one or two openings—not a hundred, like Hamlet.

The result, for Ibsen, is that his works have been played by the leading actors of the West in all decades of the twentieth century, my point being not just that these are plays that act well and allow stars to shine, but that Ibsen writes characters that can be projected as roles across the footlights (or whatever). Where a character is complete as presented to the mind's eye and the mind's ear of a reader, a role is presented to the actual eyes and ears of an audience. Now in Ibsen, as in Pirandello, we often see the characters themselves doing some role playing. Thus, Nora plays the role of a doll in a husband's doll's house. Hedda Gabler is first seen playing the role of a man: her pistol-packing father, the general. And if this is to make Ibsen too much of a Pirandellian, let me invoke Plato who proposes that we see only shadow play and not directly what is shadowed. Ibsen offers the immortal shadows of the theatre—actors playing the roles of beings who themselves quite often are playing roles.

Of course you don't need an actor to create a role-playing character. *Brand*, and this is early Ibsen, plays a single and all too single-minded role. Though *Brand* can be acted, it is, I think, no better for being acted. In the tradition of Byron and Goethe's *Faust*, it is drama in natural settings, not theatrical settings—in scenes, that is, not scenery. *Peer Gynt* is the classic role-player, but though the author, by his directions, sees the story in natural settings, a *Drang nach Theater* is also felt. Mephistopheles in Goethe's *Faust* is also a classic role-player, and one feels in all his scenes that same *Drang nach Theater*. Faust himself is a character like Prospero and *Brand* who offers the actor only so much and fails to reach out, as a role does, to the audience (which consequently has to eavesdrop on him). Mephistopheles and Peer are roles, and as such, call out to actors. And indeed actors—our greatest actors—have responded to that call.

Let me insert a thought here on the somewhat controversial topic of Ibsen's turn, in mid-life, from verse to prose. I have never been satisfied with his own explanation, which was little more than that one must heed Georg Brandes and be modern, which is to say prosaic. My dissatisfaction with that sentiment has often led me to wish that Ibsen had stuck to the kind of verse he wrote so delightfully in *Peer Gynt*. But the topic has other aspects. Ibsen did not turn to the flatly naturalistic kind of drama Brandes was thinking of. He switched to the highly theatrical and, yes, highly artificial dramaturgy of the French well-made play. He turned, that is to say, to something decidedly more histrionic. One of the final glories of this later phase of his was the creation of such characters as Nora Helmer and Rebecca West, Dr. Rank and Halvard Solness, inconceivable in a play such as *Brand* or even *Peer Gynt*. It isn't that this prose can do more than that verse, but that the prose is part of a complex (character, milieu, tone) that constitutes a far more expressive form of psychological theatre. Vine leaves in the hair or harps in the air belong, to be sure, to tragic verse. That is why their place in *Hedda Gabler* or *The Master Builder* is, to say the least, marginal, an echo, a whisper.

Verse overstates, prose understates. The modern middle-aged Ibsenite discourse is a prose of understatement, which will reach the end of the road in Samuel Beckett half a century later. People in *Brand* say the maximum, in *Ghosts* or *The Wild Duck* the minimum. Sentences are short. They may even be broken off. Silences are awesome and full of juice. In Rosmersholm, by clenching her fists and wringing her hands, Rebecca West acknowledges that her former lover turns out to have been her father. The theme, one may say, is Greek tragedy, but there will be no messenger speech and no choral ode, no song and dance.

Prose is lack of poetry, or at least lack of verbal fullness. Fullness—plenitude, if you will—is achieved in Ibsen by the combination of this understating prose with the overstating theatricality of Scribean plot. Thus the dry, reserved, tight-lipped talk has everything to do with the dramaturgy of shock and explosion I have just cited. The climactic fire in *Ghosts* is a commonplace of

Victorian fiction and drama. But it was customarily handled with the grandiose rhetoric that had trickled down from tragic verse. Balzac used that rhetoric. Dickens used it. Ibsen did not use it. On the contrary, it is possible, then, that Ibsen—the middle-aged Ibsen of the so-called modern plays—means more to theatre audiences than to readers, not to mention scholarly diggers into his text or searchers for his sources of inspiration. But what do we mean when we say "means more"? What is the meaning, here, of the word *meaning*?

At Shakespeare's quadri-centennial years ago, I asked a University of California audience: "What has Shakespeare meant?" What I had in mind was that critics and scholars are apt to announce their discovery of what Shakespeare really means, but what Shakespeare *has* meant over the years to readers and audiences is something else again. You can check what he meant to Dryden and Johnson, to Voltaire and Victor Hugo, to Goethe, to Tolstoy ... Oh dear, yes, he has meant different things at different times and in different places. And one can get a pretty good idea of what he seems to have meant to whole generations. One certainly discovers he did not mean to our forebears what Prof. So-and-So now says he really means.

Now if the great playwright means different things to critics of different times and places, to a lesser degree he also means different things in different stage productions. To a still lesser degree, a play will mean something different in every performance of the same production, not only because the performances differ, but because the audience changes nightly. This has been deftly stated in the critic Aurélio Weiss's rhetorical question: "Quel serait l'effet et le sort du drame sans la collaboration active des spectateurs, sans le développement, l'interprétation, et le sens qui'ils doivent lui donner?" Note the sense which this critic gives to the word *spectateur*. The spectator is not seen as a fellow critic in search of "what Ibsen really meant" but as one who is communing with actors of Ibsen and responding to them.

Here we come to the question: *Where* is a playwright's meaning located? And I am suggesting that a principal locus is the spectator's experience of the theatrical event. I am assuming that the import, yes, the meaning, of any literature, including dramatic literature, resides in its power, its impact, if you will, and thus does not repose in any statement it may seem to make or any philosophy it may be seen to embody.

At the head of the last movement of his last string quartet, Beethoven wrote "Muss es sein? Es muss sein." Must it be? It must be. And a flat-footed critic could view this as a summing-up and therefore the meaning of the music that follows. Those, however, who listen to the music, and give themselves to it—a participating audience—have an experience transcending by far the simple realization that something has to be, implicit in the words "Es muss sein."

Many Ibsen commentators have missed this to me fundamental point, and have looked only for statements for positions taken on social or ideological grounds. Thus *A Doll's House* is taken as a feminist statement and the critic's view of feminism determines whether he (or she) accepts the play or rejects it. But a critic who is willing to enter into a strong performance of the play, on the other hand, will come away with much more than an opinion on "the woman question," the experience is so much more than merely cerebral. Incidentally, I doubt that Ibsen is agreeing with Nora as she slams the door on her husband and abandons her children. He is only conferring dramatic definition and inevitability on the incident. Muss es sein? Es muss sein.

Am I placing too much emphasis on performance? I have argued that the reader's experience of a great play has its own validity and completeness. Hamlet lives both in the study and on the stage, if not in the same way. And to be sure the scholarly reader of Ibsen may ferret out many things that the theatre spectator will miss—both in the text itself and in the background of the text, whether in the author's life or in the literature of the time. And after all, this is not an either/or choice. You can be both a reader and a spectator. But it would seem that at a certain point, Ibsen did feel the need of theatre and actors and hence of spectators, and gave himself to them, asking us, his audience, to give ourselves in return. Thus it is reasonable to ask ourselves not only to read the words *Muss es sein? Es muss sein*, but also to listen to the music. When we do so, its impact will also be its import. This impact cannot be exactly measured or fully accounted for. If a writer refutes an opinion of ours we can sum the transaction up. *A Doll's House* seen as a feminist tract can be refuted—and was—in a story by Strindberg: one opinion drives another out, 10 minus 10 is zero. But if Ibsen is not agreeing with Nora when she walks out, he is not agreeing with Strindberg, either. He is telling what would happen in the circumstances described. And he is telling it dramatically in a narrative that offers itself theatrically to me, to you, to his audience. He does not even resist the sensationalism inherent in theatre. He exploits it in a dramaturgy of shock and explosion. *A Doll's House* was not only *heard* round the world, it was a shot, a *gunshot* heard round the world.

There are historical reasons to refer this dramaturgy back to Eugene Scribe, a minor playwright. But they wouldn't surprise Sophocles, a major playwright. *Oedipus Rex* is the classic drama of shocking, explosive secrets. Bombs hadn't been invented yet but one goes off, in Sophocles' play, every time a secret is released. In Sophocles, as in Ibsen, fatality hovers over the whole action not just as an idea but as a complex of feelings and sentiments. So, over the many, many years, what has Sophocles meant? Or Shakespeare? Or Beethoven? Or Ibsen? All have left interesting statements behind them, contributing something to our edification, though not much that had not been said by lesser talents or more philosophic minds. What they have contributed, which is unique, is a large number of large experiences to, in the end, a very large number of people.

What, we might ask, do such experiences, if we add them up, amount to? A hard question. Again, we have no measuring rod. But I would suggest that what these experiences contribute to and become a part of is civilization. They capture, they constitute, the "quality of life." For the drama, the theatre, cannot do the wonderful things that were proposed by modern playwrights from Schiller to Shaw (and very much including Ibsen. Words from his 1898 after-dinner speech come to mind: "The task always before my mind has been to advance our country and . . . to lift the people to a higher plane"). None of the arts can really be redemptive and transformative in the way the prophets and poets of the eighteenth and nineteenth centuries often hoped. None of them will save your soul or change your government. They will neither revolutionize nor reform you. But, in some degree, they can civilize you. Or enhance the life of your already civilized self.

In our time, the twentieth and now the twenty-first century, civilization—specifically, our Western civilization—has come under attack. And it has been an attack not just politically from the East but also culturally from would-be radical scholars here at home in the West. A foundation stone of Western civilization is the great individual, the great poet, composer, painter. The would-be radical critic denies his existence, affirming that the master builders of the West were all Halvard Solnesses or worse, rotten with guilt and hideously inadequate. It is true of course, that Ibsen took the hero down a peg or two. Already in *Peer Gynt* he had created the modern anti-hero and counter-Faust. But this is civilization's self-criticism. And he himself, I would like to affirm, was a giant in an era of giants: it was the time of Tolstoy and Dostoevsky, Zola and Nietzsche, not to call the roll of the sisters arts, Cézanne and Van Gogh, Brahms and Gustav Mahler.

I am raising big issues and must regretfully leave them up in the air. Let me close with a personal reminiscence. My post-graduate studies at Yale in 1939–41 began and ended with Thomas Carlyle's *Heroes and Hero Worship*, a book in which the Scottish sage called Shakespeare the greatest of intellects and the Hero as Poet. In the twentieth century, that view went out of fashion, only to return just the other day, in the twenty-first century, signed by Harold Bloom. Thank you, Harold. What I have been saying is that Ibsen was the Hero as Playwright.

TANYA THRESHER

"Vinløv i håret": *The Relationship Between Women, Language, and Power in Ibsen's* Hedda Gabler

The difficulty Ibsen's women experience accessing the dominant male discourse finds its most acute example in *Hedda Gabler* (1890), the play in which Ibsen's dramatic dialogue is at its most condensed and circumlocution is the dominant narrative technique.[1] The paucity of Hedda's words has been a matter of critical concern since the very inception of the play. In an 1891 review of *Hedda Gabler*, Edmund Gosse stated that

> I will dare to say that I think in this instance Ibsen has gone
> perilously far in his desire for rapid and concise expression. The
> *stichomythia* of the Greek and French tragedians was lengthy in
> comparison with this unceasing display of hissing conversational
> fireworks, fragments of sentences without verbs, clauses that come
> to nothing, adverbial exclamations and cryptic interrogatories. It
> would add, I cannot but think, to the lucidity of the play if some
> one character were permitted occasionally to express himself at
> moderate length ... (5)

While Gosse considers the entire play, other critics, like James McFarlane, focus on the central character herself, noting that the protagonist "must surely be one of the least eloquent heroines in the whole of the world's

From *Modern Drama* 51, no. 1 (Spring 2008): 73–83. Copyright © 2008 *Modern Drama*.

dramatic literature" (285). In line with McFarlane, Else Høst, in her 1958 monograph about the piece, considers that Hedda is

> [a]ntagelig verdenslitteraturens mest ordknappe heltinne. . . . ikke det beskjedneste tilløp til en monolog er henne bevilget for å tolke sin indre verden; bare ved et par anledninger bryter hun med styk-kets rolige konversasjonstone. Det aller mest av hva hun sier, går inn som nødvendige ledd i en høyst ordinær replikkveksling om daglidagse materier. Som en ren unntagelse faller en avstikkende formulering henne i munnen: symboluttrykket "vinløv i håret."

> [most likely the most reticent heroine in world literature. . . . [N]ot the most modest hint of a monologue is granted her in order to interpret her inner world: only in a couple of instances does she break with the calm conversational tone of the piece. Most of what she says appears as necessary links in a highly ordinary exchange of words about everyday matters. A pure exception is the conspicuous formulation that falls from her mouth: the symbolic expression "vine leaves in the hair."][2](197)

Hedda's lack of garrulity is striking, but, nevertheless, the general's daughter shows an acute awareness of the power of words, knowing that they carry with them an emancipatory potential. Words hold the possibility of liberation from the ennui of bourgeois married existence and offer Hedda the opportunity to control the fate of other people, something for which she has a strong desire, as she admits to Fru Elvsted—*"jeg vil for en eneste gang i mit liv ha' magt over en menneskeskæbne* [for once in my life I want to have power over a human destiny] (*Hedda, Hundreårsutgave* 11: 355).[3] In spite of Hedda's consciousness of the manipulative potential of words, she nevertheless fails to negotiate that potential adequately and ultimately chooses to appropriate silence as a means of challenging her position within the patriarchal order. This choice results from her comprehension of the emptiness of her words and of her resulting inability to attain the comradeship defined by Løvborg, an understanding facilitated by the death of Løvborg and the suspension of her belief in vine-leaves. Hedda's basic misunderstanding of language as a negotiation of power and her ultimate choice of silence are a stage in Ibsen's analysis of the mechanisms of meaning, an analysis originating most clearly in *Vildanden [The Wild Duck]* (1884) and culminating in *Når vi døde vågner [When We Dead Awaken]* (1899). This analysis, in turn, is closely connected to the self-reflexive nature of Ibsen's works and further highlights the aesthetic self-consciousness that situates the playwright more as a modernist than a realist.[4]

From the moment Hedda enters the stage, the play develops into a series of linguistic attempts on the part of the heroine at controlling reality and a growing realization that the relationship between language and reality is conditioned by the dominant ideology, in this case patriarchy. Hedda tries repeatedly, and with some success, to gain power through words and uses them to form an effective defensive barrier between herself and the Tesman family, a family that, for the general's daughter, as Ibsen wrote in a letter to Kristine Steen, "*danner tilsammen et helheds—og enhedsbillede. De har fælles tankegang, fælles erindringer, fælles livssyn. For Hedda står de som en mod hendes grundvæsen rettet fiendtlig og fremmed magt* [together forms a complete and unifying picture. They have a common way of thinking, common memories, a common view of life. For Hedda, they stand against her essential being as one hostile and alien power]" (*Hundreårsutgave* 18: 280). Hedda's rejection of familial affiliation comes about not only in the sustained use of "Gabler" as a surname but also in her refusing to use a personalized form of address for Tante Julle; in her verbally rejecting that epitome of Tesmanesque domesticity, Tesman's embroidered slippers (*Hedda, Hundreårsutgave* 11: 305–06); and, finally, in her purposely, as she later admits to Assessor Brack, insulting Tante Julle by pretending to believe her newly acquired hat belongs to the maid Berthe. In these instances, Hedda uses words to avoid becoming party to a social contract and to reinforce her social position as a member of the upper class, something that is increasingly threatened by her surroundings.

In order to take control of surroundings she increasingly finds "*tarvelige* [wretched]" (*Hedda, Hundreårsutgave* 11: 337), Hedda resorts to the coercive potential of words. Initially, this is apparent as Hedda, through simple questions, successfully elicits information from Thea concerning her current situation. In spite of an acknowledgement that she formerly feared General Gabler's daughter, an initial reluctance to talk with her, and a clear indication (in Hedda's misnaming her Thora) that the two have not been intimate, Thea willingly reveals to Hedda details of her relationship to Løvborg. Resisting Hedda's initial request, "*[f]ortæll mig nu lidt om hvorledes De har det i hjemmet* [now tell me a little about how it is at home]" (315), and her later insistence that "*nu skal du fortælle mig alting—således som det er* [now you must tell me everything—just as it really is]" (317), Thea finally agrees not merely to take part in the conversation but moreover to accept a kind of interrogation, saying, "*Ja, så får du spørge da* [Yes, then you can ask]" (317). In spite of some hesitation and speaking brokenly, Thea does, then, admit to Hedda the details of her life at home and the shocking (at least, for Hedda) fact that she has left her husband in order to follow Løvborg into town.

The linguistic control Hedda exerts over Thea in this instance has its precedent in her conversations with Løvborg, conversations that are verbal

enactments, or theatricalizations, of his sexual exploits under the distant sur-
veillance of General Gabler. Hedda and Løvborg self-consciously replicate
these earlier conversations when they browse through a photograph album of
Hedda and Tesman's wedding trip and talk of their earlier relationship, a relationship Hedda remembers as one of "*to gode kammerater. To rigtige fortrolige
venner* [two good comrades. Two really intimate friends]" (*Hedda, Hundreårsutgave* 11: 347). Charles R. Lyons underscores the importance of Hedda's
interaction with Løvborg in the Tesman living room, as it is here that

> we see both the mask, Hedda's pretense of showing Løvborg the
> photos performed for Tesman and Brack, and a rare honesty of
> language as Hedda relives the earlier experience. In Hedda's imagi-
> nation, the experience she realized in these concealed conversations
> seems to remain the most vital segment of her life. At least, we see
> her engaged with the memory of a moment from the past with a
> greater display of energy than at any other point in the text. (106)

While Hedda recalls the earlier conversations with Løvborg as "*noget
skønt, noget lokkende,—noget modigt synes jeg der var over—over denne løn-
domsfulde fortrolighed—dette kammeratskab* [something beautiful, something
tempting/seductive—I believe there was something courageous about—
about this secret intimacy—this comradeship]" (*Hedda, Hundreårsutgave* 11:
347), Løvborg is conscious of the power Hedda held over him:

> LØVBORG Å Hedda—hvad var der dog for en magt i Dem, som
> tvang mig til at bekende sligt noget?
> HEDDA Tror De, det var en magt i mig?
> LØVBORG Ja, hvorledes skal jeg ellers forklare mig det? Og alle
> disse—disse omsvøbsfulde spørgsmål, som De gjorde mig–
> HEDDA Og som De så inderlig godt forstod–
> LØVBORG At De kunde sidde og spørge således! Ganske frejdigt!
> HEDDA Omsvøbsfuldt, må jeg be.
> LØVBORG Ja, men frejdigt alligevel. Spørge mig ud om—om alt
> sligt noget!
> LØVBORG Oh, Hedda—what kind of power was in you that
> forced me to confess such things?
> HEDDA Do you think there was a power in me?
> LØVBORG Well, how else can I explain it? And all those—those
> evasive questions you asked me–
> HEDDA And which you understood so well–
> LØVBORG That you could sit and ask like that! Quite boldly!

HEDDA I had to ask evasively.
LØVBORG Yes, but boldly all the same. Interrogate me about—
about such things!]

(347–48)

As in the situation with Thea, Hedda was able, in this instance, to extort
sensitive information through careful questioning, giving Løvborg the
impression of participating in some kind of religious confession, an impression intensified by the use of the verbs *"at bekende"* and *"at skrifte,"* both of
which mean to confess, in a religious sense. The implication that Hedda
exerted a spiritual force is further strengthened in Løvborg's later inquiry as
to whether it was not *"som om De vilde ligesom tvætte mig ren,—når jeg tyed til
dem i bekendelse?* [as if you somehow wanted to absolve me—when I turned
to you and confessed]" (348). For a woman whose acknowledged desire is to
have power over another person's fate, this kind of expiation through story-
telling must certainly have been attractive to Hedda.

Due to their content, Hedda's intimate conversations with Løvborg
are clear transgressions of the moral boundaries of correct behaviour for a
nineteenth-century middle-class woman. Similar in transgressive potential
is Hedda's persuading Løvborg the alcoholic to take a glass of punch, per-
suasion masterfully effected through the revelation of Thea's concern for
her friend, which necessarily calls into question Løvborg's understanding
of the comradeship based on trust and open dialogue he believes the two
share. Likewise, the incident with Julle's hat and that when the heroine
says she longs to burn Thea's hair are evidence of a dislocation of words and
moral responsibility characteristic of Hedda, something that the heroine
transfers to Tesman with apparent ease when she convinces him to overlook
the ethical implications of destroying a colleague's work by admitting she
burned the manuscript due to her perception of his jealousy of Løvborg.
Tesman's willing complicity is strengthened by the suggestion that Hedda
is pregnant, and while his guilty conscience may ultimately inform his decision to piece together Løvborg's manuscript with Thea after the author's
death, he nevertheless fails, during the course of the play, to disclose the
true fate of the original piece of work. The power of words to hide reality
is confirmed in Tesman's rash conclusion that Hedda acted out of burning
passion for him, a passion associated with socially sanctioned love or the
marriage contract.

An alternative to the marriage contract is offered in the comradeship
between Løvborg and Thea, whose relationship best exemplifies the emancipatory potential of language and, in particular, speech. While publishing
Løvborg's manuscript offers him the possibility of reinstating himself in

society and will permit him a social victory, it is the act of conversing openly with others that, according to Løvborg, defines *"kammerater,"* the comrades of the future outlined in the new manuscript. Ibsen elucidates the relevance of comradeship in his notes for the play:

> Ejlert Løvborgs tanke er at der må skaffes tilveje et kammer-atskabsforhold mellem man og kvinde, hvoraf det sande åndelige menneske kan fremgå. Det øvrige, som to bedriver, ligger udenfor som det uvæsentlige. Dette er det, som omgivelserne ikke forstår. Han er for dem en udsvævende person. I det indre ikke.

> [Ejlert Løvborg's idea is that a relationship of comradeship between men and women has to be created, from which the truly intellectual person may result. Whatever else two people may engage in is insignificant. This is what the people around him do not understand. He is, for them, a debauched person. Not on the inside.] (509)

Classifying comradeship between the sexes as *"Redningstanken!* [the rescue thought]," Ibsen further states in his notes that *"[d]et nye i E.L.s bog er læren om udvikling på grundlag af kammeratskab mellem mand og kvinde* [the new element in E.L.'s book is the tenet about development based on comradeship between man and woman]" (512). This development is closely associated with intellectual cooperation in the draft of the play, in which Hedda jealously imagines Løvborg and Thea working together in the Elvsted house (468). Hedda's hasty rejection of Tesman's offer to work similarly with him is evidence of her perception of her husband's unsuitability for such a relationship, something that the final version of the play readdresses when Thea and Tesman embark on recreating the lost manuscript in the memory of Løvborg.

In stark contrast to his relationship to Hedda, Løvborg characterizes his relationship to Thea as *"to rigtige kammerater. Vi tror ubetinget på hinan-den. Og så kan vi sidde og tale så frejdigt sammen—*[two real comrades. We believe unconditionally in each other. And then we can sit and talk so boldly together—]" (*Hedda, Hundreårsutgave* 11: 350). Such an open dialogue has, for Thea, turned her into a *"virkeligt mennekse* [real human being]" (319),[5] as Løvborg has taught her to think not only by reading with her but also by talking about all sorts of things. Thea's desire to maintain her new-found status is revealed as she sets about piecing together Løvborg's manuscript after his death, for in recreating the object she has described as *"barnet* [the child]" (373), she is reproducing the consummation of the comradeship she earlier enjoyed with Løvborg, this time with Tesman.

This comradeship with Thea is, perhaps, an idealization on the part of Løvborg, and he later comes to regard their relationship in a different manner, claiming that "*[d]et er livsmodet og livstrodsen, som hun har knækket i mig* [she has broken the courage to live and to defy life in me]" (373). Such an ideal comradeship with Hedda, on the other hand, is unattainable, as talking with the general's daughter is an activity filled with "*omsvøb* [circumlocution]," a trait that affects her potential to become a true comrade and results in an inability to act. Løvborg suggests that with an openness of language comes action, by saying of Thea and her relationship to her comrade that "*[o]g så er det handlingens mod, som hun har, fru Tesman!* [and then she has the courage to act, Mrs. Tesman!]" (350). The inference that it is actions that, indeed, speak louder than words is supported by Thea's blatant disregard for what people might say regarding her abandonment of her husband in favour of Løvborg. To Hedda's question, "*Men hvad tror du så folk vil sige om dig, Thea?* [But then what do you think people will say about you, Thea?]," Thea replies, "*De får i guds navn sige, hvad de vil. For jeg har ikke gjort andet end jeg måtte gøre* [In God's name, they can say what they like. Because I haven't done anything other than what I had to do]" (319).

While Hedda's fear of what other people might say about her reveals her preoccupation with the spoken word and her awareness of language as a constraining, disciplinary mechanism, it is, nevertheless, Thea who comprehends the complex relationship between words and actions. After Hedda has manipulated Løvborg into drinking punch by causing him to doubt the comradeship the two share, Thea asks of the general's daughter, "*Hvad er det du siger! Hvad er det du gør!* [What are you saying! What are you doing!]" (352). The clear association between word and deed—and hence the relationship of words to reality—is something Hedda has been indoctrinated by her peers to deny, as is most clearly evidenced when she threatens Løvborg with her pistols at his suggestion that they change their relationship into something physical. Hedda's motivation, as stated by the general's daughter herself, is the "*overhængende fare for at der vilde komme virkelighed ind i forholdet* [imminent danger that reality would enter into the relationship]" (348).

The relationship between reality and language is at its most dislocated in the motif of the "*vinløv i håret* [vine leaves in the hair]," an expression used to voice Hedda's vision of Løvborg once he has supposedly "*fåt magten over sig selv igen* [gained power over himself again]" (355) and become "*en fri mand for alle sine dage* [a free man for all his days]" (355). The expression, which is entirely absent from Ibsen's drafts for the piece and appears only six times in the entire play, contrasts sharply with Hedda's other language, particularly if we interpret the image as a Romantic one and consider Hedda's absolute disgust with words such as "*elsker* [love/loves (vb.)]," which she refers to as "*det klissete ord* [that sentimental word]" (331).[6] The vine-leaf expression occurs twice at the close of Act Two as Hedda explains to Thea her vision of Løvborg at Brack's soirée, reading his manuscript to her husband, and it is repeated, again to Thea, the following morning. When Tesman returns home, Hedda uses the phrase once more to ask her husband about the events of the previous night. Subsequently, as Hedda hears from Brack about the actual events of the party, she surmises that Løvborg did not have vine leaves in his hair. The final mention of the image occurs as Løvborg questions Hedda about her vision of his beautiful death.

Hedda has established herself from the outset of the play as uninterested, to say the least, in the natural world—conscious of the withering leaves outside, she is dismayed at the overabundance of cut flowers in the villa, for example, and requests that the curtains be drawn in order to block out the sunlight. Likewise, her physical aversion to her pregnancy adds to the incongruity of a natural image like vine leaves. Moreover, as John Northam points out, Ibsen does not fully develop the imagery of vine leaves in the play, something unusual in such a well-crafted piece, in which there is a subtle, gradual exposition of, for example, the curtain or hair motifs (70). Rather, the vine leaves occur abruptly at the end of Act Two, something that, in association with Ibsen's notes for the play, which say that there is a "*dyb poesi* [deep poetry]" in Hedda, Northam interprets as an indication of a "vision, a set of values in Hedda that is, for her, absolute, and therefore unchangeable" (501). These values, according to Northam, oppose the social imperatives that force Hedda into conformity with the conventions of societClearly the vine-leaf imagery represents some kind of ideology in Hedda and may constitute part of her underlying deep poetry, but it remains difficult to assign it an essential nature, as the image remains under-developed and Hedda easily rejects it. After hearing from Brack the details of Løvborg's drunken exploits, Hedda admonishes Løvborg in Act Three to shoot himself beautifully. Løvborg responds, "*I skjønhed. (Smiler.) Med vinløv i håret, som De før i tiden tænkte Dem*—[In beauty. (*Smiles.*) With vine leaves in my hair, as you imagined in the past]," to which Hedda replies with the final mention of vine leaves in the piece, "*Å nei—Vinløvet,—det tror jeg ikke længer på. Men i skønhed alligevel!* [Oh no—Vine leaves—I don't believe in that any more. But in beauty nevertheless!" (375). Hedda's renunciation of the vine imagery lessens the critical temptation to invest it with a sophisticated interpretation by way of Euripides's *The Bacchae* or readings of the Dionysus myth. Rather, as Lyons has said about such attempts, "the text itself gives us no evidence that she [Hedda] commands this kind of knowledge or that this paradigm infuses her language. Hedda identifies and celebrates Løvborg's rebellion, not its ideology" (87).

Hedda's ultimate rejection of the vine-leaf imagery is concomitant with the weakening power of her words, as, after all, Løvborg does not leave her with the intention of shooting himself beautifully at all but rather returns to Madame Diana's boudoir in hopes of retrieving his manuscript. Moreover, it clearly illustrates Hedda's evolving distrust of the liberating and poetical potential of words. Such a belief in the power of words to liberate, if we consider the fact that Hedda and Thea are the only characters who accept the vine-leaf image unquestioningly, appears to be female gendered and related to a willingness to transgress the limitations of patriarchy. Both Tesman and Brack respond with questions when Hedda uses the vine-leaf imagery in their presence (418, 421). They are representatives of a socially sanctioned use of language and uphold the dominant ideology through Tesman's written documentation of history and Brack's verbal interpretation of the law. Løvborg's use of the vine-leaf expression, while referring to Hedda's own and uttered perhaps ironically (as the stage directions may indicate), is evidence (along with the manuscript) of his comprehension, at least, of the desire to test the limits of the patriarchal ideology. Nevertheless, as his manuscript and earlier discussions of comrades suggest, he finds transgressive potential and an associated movement towards becoming a true human being in the practice of talking openly.

Unlike Løvborg, Hedda Gabler is unwilling to transgress the socially sanctioned linguistic indoctrination that has effectively taught her silence. While Hedda's vigilance with regard to open expression is shown in the way she rarely delivers simple straightforward statements but rather frames her utterances with questions in order to first ascertain the opinions of her conversational partner, her final appropriation of silence disrupts the disciplinary mechanism that society has taught her. Her relationship to silence is foreshadowed in the opening dialogue of the play, in which a brief interaction between Tante Julle and Berthe encapsulates the myth that is the general's daughter and underscores the distance between the myth and the reality that is the Tesman family. This dialogue frames Hedda in silence, for, while she is the topic of the conversation, she is absent—a situation paralleling that of the end of the drama. Moreover, her silence is tacitly connected to her newly acquired social status as Tesman's wife, as Julle and the maid mention that Hedda is still asleep in the marital bed with her spouse (295). Supporting her silencing within marriage is Hedda's own unwillingness to talk openly of her pregnancy or of any aspect of her sexuality; indeed, she actively tries to silence Tesman, when he begins to tell Tante Julle of the fullness of her figure, by interrupting him three times while moving towards the glass veranda, the space that symbolizes her desire for freedom (391). Likewise, the discussion with Brack regarding her wedding trip tacitly utilizes metaphor, here the train journey and the possibility of a third person's joining a married couple in their compartment, to suggest an extra-marital affair. As Lyons indicates, "This exchange demonstrates the skillful control with which both Hedda and Brack manage their sexual references within the safety of an almost-neutralized vocabulary" (123).

The careful neutralization of words has slowly relegated Hedda to a position of silence. The dangerous potential of such a position is most evident in Brack's silence regarding ownership of the pistol that fatally wounds Løvborg, for Brack's silence will place Hedda forever in his power, a power he intends to use for sexual exploitation. Hedda's diminishing power in this instance is underscored by Brack's increasingly intimate forms of address, as he switches from the formal "Hedda Gabler" and "*Fru Tesman* [Mrs. Tesman]" to "Hedda" and "*kæreste Hedda* [dear Hedda]." While Brack's silence with regard to the pistol is the most opaquely threatening, Hedda's social subordination through silence is evident throughout the play. Her situation as mistress of the Falk Villa, which is itself a spatial representation of silence due to its association with death and absence, has resulted from her desire to break silence with Tesman as he accompanies her home one evening (336). Her status as Tesman's wife is likewise the outcome of her silence regarding her sexual attraction to Løvborg, a silence the draft of the play intensifies, when Løvborg explains that he pursued a relationship with Thea as a result of hearing nothing from Hedda: "*Men da jeg så aldrig mere fik høre fra Dem,— aldrig fik et ord til svar på mine breve*—[But when I never heard from you again–never got a word in answer to my letters–]" (452). Hedda's response to this accusation—"*Det er uforsigtigt at gi' noget skriftlig fra sig. Og desuden—til slut—så svared jeg Dem da tilstrækkelig tydeligt—i handling* [It is not careful to give something written from oneself. And besides—in the end—I answered you sufficiently clearly—in action]" (452)—shows yet again Hedda's propensity to dissociate word and action.

It is Hedda's final choice to appropriate silence that allows her to re-establish the connection between word and deed and effectively neutralize the masterful threat Brack poses. Moreover, this new silence transforms her initial silence regarding her true feelings for Løvborg, something that she confesses to be her "*argeste feighet* [bitterest cowardice]" (349), into an act of courage. Her choice is made as she refuses to say, without any real coercion on Brack's part, that the pistol found on Løvborg was stolen from her. For a woman who, in the past, has shown a disregard for the truth-value of words and used them to manipulate and control others, this seems an all-too-easy confession, especially once we understand the dire consequences of it. While we cannot eliminate the possibility of a correspondence between Hedda's uncharacteristic insistence on the truth and an unwillingness on her part to surrender her past and/or her masculine power (of which the pistol is the most obvious symbol), Hedda's choice of silence, made all the more apparent by the playing of a wild dance melody on the piano, her disappearance into the back room, and her line "*[h]erefter skal jeg være stille* [after this I will be quiet]" (392) provide us with Ibsen's most provoking challenge. These words are not, in fact, the last time we hear from Hedda, for she actually delivers two more lines, the final one being her suggestion to Brack that he continue hoping to be entertained in her house as the cock of the walk, a suggestion abruptly broken by the sound of the gunshot. Likewise, her erasure from the stage does not denote the end of the conversation that is Hedda. Rather, it encourages Brack, as the representative of patriarchy, to search for a meaning behind words, something evident if we take the suicide as a defiant negation of his earlier assertion that "*Sligt noget siger man. Men man gør det ikke* [One says such things. But one does not do them]" (390), and his subsequent final line "*Men, gud sig forbarme,—sligt noget gør man da ikke!* [But, good lord, one doesn't do such things!]" (393).

With Hedda's final action Ibsen appeals to his audience to investigate the correspondence between words and actions, those elements that constitute the very foundation of theatrical art. At the same time, Hedda's theatrical erasure from the stage signals his fundamental distrust of the linguistic signifying system and reveals his "deep-seated skepticism with regard to our possibilities of knowing another human being" (Moi, 34). Hedda's final act is, thus, both a liberation from the absurdity of existence that tells us more than her words ever could and a deafening interrogation of the limits of the linguistic medium in relationship to otherness—an affirmation, thus, of the unspeakable beauty of vine leaves in one's hair.

NOTES

1. Charles R. Lyons gives a detailed account of the rhetorical strategy of circumlocution; see 110–35.

2. All translations from Norwegian, including those from Ibsen's plays, are my own in order to ensure the most literal translation of the original.

3. In Ibsen's draft for the piece, Hedda wants power over a person's "*sind* [mind]" (460) rather than fate. This strengthens her ambition for intellectual stimulation and offers a possible further explanation as to her choice and subsequent disappointment in marriage.

4. Recent Ibsen scholarship has sought to re-evaluate Ibsen's relationship to modernism. Atle Kittang's *Ibsens heroisme* and Toril Moi's *Henrik Ibsen and the Birth of Modernism* are two apt examples.

5. The importance of being a human being as opposed to a man or woman has been a recurring theme in Ibsen's work since *Et Dukkehjem*, in which Nora responds to Helmer's accusation that "*Du er først og fremst hustru og moder* [You are first and foremost a wife and mother]," with "*Det tror jeg ikke længere på. Jeg tror, at jeg er først*

*og fremst et menneske, jeg likesåvel som du,—eller ialdfald, at jeg skal forsøge på at bli'e
det* [I don't believe that any longer. I believe that I am first and foremost a human
being just like you—or at any rate that I should try to become one]" (*Hundreårsutgave* 8: 359).

6. In the draft of the play, Hedda is much more assertive in her rejection of
love, deriding Løvborg when he suggests she loves Tesman and explaining that she
believes love does not really exist. Of love, she states that *"Jeg tror det er bare noget,
som folk finder på. Og som de går omkring og snakker om* [I think it is just something
people make up. And that they go around and talk about]" (*Hedda, Hundreårsutgave*
11: 448–49).

WORKS CITED

Gosse, Edmund. "Ibsen's New Drama." Rev. of *Hedda Gabler. Fortnightly Review* ns 49 (1
    Jan.-1 June 1891): 4–13.

Høst, Else. "Utdrag fra Hedda Gabler (1958). [Excerpt from Hedda Gabler (1958)]" In *Et
    skjær av uvilkårlig skjønnhet. Om Henrik Ibsens Hedda Gabler. [A Touch of Spontaneous
    Beauty. About Henrik Ibsen's* Hedda Gabler]. Ed. Anne Marie Rekdal. Gjøvik: LNU,
    Cappelen Akademisk, 2001. 85–91.

Ibsen, Henrik. Draft of *Hedda Gabler. Hundreårsutgave: Henrik Ibsens Samlede Verker.* Vol. 11.
    Ed. Francis Bull, Halvdan Koht, and Didrik Arup Siep. Oslo: Gyldendal Norsk Forlag,
    1928–1957. 402–95.

Et dukkehjem. Ibsen, Hundreårsutgave Vol. 8. 271–364.

———. *Hedda Gabler.* Ibsen, *Hundreårsutgave* Vol. 11 261–556.

———. Notes to *Hedda Gabler.* Ibsen, *Hundreårsutgave* Vol. 11 496–556.

———. "Til Kristine Steen [To Kristine Steen]." Ibsen, *Hundreårsutgave* Vol. 18. 279–80.

Kittang, Atle. *Ibsens heroisme.* Oslo: Gyldendal, 2002.

Lyons, Charles R. *Hedda Gabler: Gender, Role, and World.* Boston: Twayne, 1990.

Northam, John. "Hedda Gabler." *Ibsen Årbok* 68/69: 60–81.

McFarlane, James. *Ibsen and Meaning.* Norwich: Norvik, 1989.

Moi, Toril. Henrik Ibsen and the Birth of Modernism: Art, Theatre, Philosophy. Oxford:
    Oxford UP, 2006.

KRISTIN BRUNNEMER

Sexuality in Henrik Ibsen's A Doll's House

In his time, Henrik Ibsen was a controversial playwright who wrote plays on taboo subjects. From banishment (*Peer Gynt*), to illegitimate children (*The Wild Duck*), to syphilis and euthanasia (*Ghosts*), to suicide (*Hedda Gabler*), Ibsen's characters occupied identities onstage that few in polite Victorian society would dare to mention. Perhaps surprisingly for modern readers, *A Doll's House*, with its plot centered on a woman named Nora who forges her father's signature, takes a loan without consulting her husband, and leaves him and her children to find herself, was considered equally shocking by its first audiences. The play was deemed so daring that, when performed in many countries, the ending was changed so that Nora returns home, finding she cannot leave Torvald or her three children so great is her love and devotion to them (Templeton 113–114). Nora's quest for her personal identity, while scandalous to some at the time, is exactly what made the play so famous—and why it continues to hold such currency as a drama today.

Critical studies of *A Doll's House* often center on the ongoing debate as to whether or not the play offers a feminist message, and whether or not Ibsen meant it to do so. Those who oppose such a feminist reading of the text often turn to Ibsen's own words on the play to the Norwegian Women's Rights League in 1898: "I thank you for the toast, but must disclaim the honor of having consciously worked for the women's rights movement. I am not even

From *Human Sexuality*, Bloom's Literary Themes, edited by Harold Bloom, pp. 9–17.
Copyright © 2009 Chelsea House Publishers.

quite clear as to just what this women's rights movement really is. To me it has seemed a problem of humanity in general" (Ibsen, quoted in Ricardson 81). Such critics favor a reading of Nora's transformation as humanist rather than feminist, and Eric Bentley, for example, argues that "the play would be just as valid were Torvald the wife and Nora the husband"(30).

Those who read the play as a feminist piece, such as Gail Finney, however, hold that Ibsen's "sensitivity to feminist issues" is revealed in "his creation of female characters" and "their rejection of a strict division between conventional masculine and feminine behavior" (92–93). Likewise, Joan Templeton contests what she calls "the *Doll's House* backlash" wherein the feminist aspects of the play are attacked on "literary grounds" under the pretext that Nora's character between act one and act three undergoes "an incomprehensible transformation" (114). Instead, Templeton argues that "[t]he power of *A Doll's House* lies not 'beyond' but within its feminism; it is a feminist Bildungspiel *par excellence*, dramatizing the protagonist's realization that she might, perhaps, be someone other than her husband's little woman" (138).

The problem, of course, could be that feminism is often difficult to define, a problem noted by bell hooks and Carmen Vasquez. Vasquez argues that feminism, unfortunately, "has come to mean anything you like [...] There are as many definitions of Feminism as there are feminists" (Vasquez qtd. in hooks 17). Thus, one scholar's humanism may be another's feminism.

Despite these debates, critics spend little time discussing Nora's transformative identity on its own terms. This is unfortunate because Nora, throughout the course of the play, illustrates many of the levels of American psychologist Abraham Maslow's hierarchy of needs. Moving through the stages of this hierarchy, from physiological elements such as safety, love and belonging, to the desire for esteem and self-actualization, Nora's character exemplifies Maslow's theory that "most behavior occur[s] in response to some kind of motivation, which [is] made up of the interplay among different needs, or drives" (Krapp 309). In her interactions with Kristine, Krogstad, Dr. Rank and, most especially, Torvald, Nora consistently shows how needs—not unconscious, internal motivations—are the key to her growing personal identity.

Abraham Maslow, discontent with psychotherapy of the 1930s, which focused rather exclusively on either Freud's psychoanalysis or B. F. Skinner's behaviorist methods, developed his theory of the hierarchy of needs as a method for understanding what motivates successful, healthy people in the development of their personalities. At the bottom of the hierarchy's scale are physiological needs, such as the need for food, water, shelter, and air. The next level of Maslow's hierarchy, titled safety, consists of the need for financial resources, health, and security. According to Maslow, only after these two stages of need have been successfully satisfied can one progress to the next levels, which consist of the need for love and belonging, the need for esteem, and the need for self-actualization (Krapp 310). Today, the hierarchy is employed in studies of human behavior and identity and even in professional fields such as advertising, marketing, and office relations.

In the first act of the play, Nora returns to her house from shopping in preparation for Christmas festivities. We learn from her early interactions with Torvald that Nora has been concerned about her family's financial situation for quite some time, in part due to her husband's bout with illness in the past. However, with Torvald's new job at the bank beginning in the New Year, the Helmer household anticipates a more stable and affluent future. As Torvald tells Nora, "Ah, it is so gratifying to know that one's gotten a safe, secure job, and with a comfortable salary" (1578). Though Maslow argued that "safety needs are relatively less important for most healthy adults under normal circumstances," there are "exceptional circumstances" that can "activate safety needs in people whose safety needs had previously been satisfied" (Krapp 310). Such is the case with Nora, whose fear for Torvald's health, and by extension her only means of financial security in late Victorian society, prompted her to forge her father's signature in order to borrow sufficient funds to take the family to Italy for Torvald's recovery.

Nora, as Maslow's theory suggests, has been unable to think of much else besides this need for safety, and to keep her attempts to satisfy it a secret from her husband. "You can imagine, of course, how this thing hangs over me," Nora tells Kristine in Act I (1584). As such, all other needs have been put on hold, and Nora details her preoccupation with safety to Kristine, explaining how she has secretly worked, skimped, and saved to pay back the loan and its attendant interest.

Nora's conversation with Kristine also reveals Nora's new and growing desire for esteem, the third level in the hierarchy of needs, which involves both "the need for self-esteem and the need for esteem from others," according to Maslow (Krapp 311). While Nora initially (and rather thoughtlessly, given Kristine's own dismal circumstances) brags to her friend of Torvald's new job, which will bring in "a huge salary and lots of commissions" (1580), she soon feels patronized by Kristine's insistence that she is "just a child" who "really know[s] so little of life's burdens" (1582). To contest this reading of herself, Nora reveals the actions she took to convey her family to Italy and thus save her husband's life. With her need for safety and security fulfilled by the promise of Torvald's new job, Nora now clearly seeks something greater than security: self-worth. Telling Kristine, of course, isn't prudent, but it furthers the plot along, bringing the play into the classic stage of complication, while revealing Nora's "need to feel that other people respect and recognize [her] as worthwhile" (Knapp 8).

However, a visit by her husband's employee Nils Krogstad soon returns Nora to the second stage in Maslow's hierarchy, reconnecting her with her long-held fears for security. Blackmailing Nora with his knowledge that she has forged her father's signature on the loan she took for the trip to Italy, Krogstad tells Nora that he will reveal her secret, thereby opening her up to legal recourse and social shame, unless she can convince Torvald to keep Krogstad at the bank. Ironically, Krogstad blackmails Nora because, he, too, is fearful about his level of security and esteem; this job, Krogstad reveals, is "the first rung" of the ladder he must climb to achieve social acceptance after tarnishing his reputation in an unnamed scandal. "My boys are growing up," he tells Nora. "For their sakes, I'll have to win back as much respect as possible" (1590). Krogstad, like Nora, has been operating at deprivation levels in Maslow's realm of security, and, as Maslow suggests, a person worried about safety and security will "focus on satisfying this need to the exclusion of all other needs, living 'almost for safety alone'" (KrappJust as Nora has set aside thoughts of legal recourse and social shame in her attempts to secure Torvald's health, so, too, has Krogstad sought this same level of security without thought for the impact his blackmail will have on Nora. For these reasons, Errol Durbach argues that "Krogstad is a mirror that throws back at Nora the reflection of a persecuted criminal in an unforgiving society [. . .] Krogstad and Nora are fellow criminals beneath skin" (78–79). Brian Johnston, likewise, recognizes that "Krogstad's determination to secure the future of his sons is no more ignoble a motive than Nora's past wishes to save her husband's life and to spare her dying father" (150). Nevertheless, Krogstad's intimidations do more than threaten Nora's safety; they terrorize her into pondering suicide as a solution (Ibsen 1619).

Significantly, *A Doll's House* also reveals Nora's desire for the third stage in Maslow's hierarchy, love and belonging, which is equally strong in the first and second acts of the play. Maslow makes a distinction between two types of love, Deprivation-Love and Being-Love: Deprivation-Love, the "essentially selfish need to give and receive affection from others," is a lower form than Being-Love, the "unselfish desire for what is best for the loved one" (Krapp 310). Nora does initially focus on Deprivation-Love, manifesting a desire to garner care and concern from her family (Knapp 310). Basking in Torvald's diminutive nicknames for her, such as "lark" and "little squirrel," Nora centers her existence on pleasing Torvald so that she, in turn, can receive the satisfaction of being desired and cherished. Likewise, Nora's interactions with her children, her "dolls," are similarly motivated. This sense of Nora's love being deprivation-based rather than unselfish is also clearly exhibited by Nora's concern that Torvald might love her less in the future, "when he stops enjoying [her] dancing and dressing up and reciting for him" (Ibsen 1583).

However, Nora's fear of this lack is so great she quickly stops herself from such thoughts: "How ridiculous! That'll never happen" (1583).

Nora also exhibits Deprivation-Love in her interactions with Dr. Rank, the Helmers' dying family friend whose love for Nora is more romantic in nature than fatherly. Nora is a rather shameless flirt when it comes to acquiring Dr. Rank's affections, and Ibsen's stage direction for Nora and Rank's scene alone together is filled with appropriately coy instructions: the actress is directed to put "both hands on his shoulders" and to hit "him lightly on the ear with [her] stockings" (1603). The dialogue of the scene is equally flirtatious, with Nora telling him to "imagine then that I'm dancing only for you" before remembering to add, "yes, and of course, for Torvald too—that's understood" (Ibsen 1603). Moreover, throughout the scene, Nora desires Rank's affections not just for her own need for friendship and intimacy, but also in hopes that Rank will ultimately be like her fantasy of an "old gentleman" whom, as she tells Kristine, she has long daydreamed will rescue her from her financial predicaments (1584). Nora's flirtations are thus quite purposeful, performed with the hope of securing "an exceptionally big favor" from Rank to help her escape Krogstad's blackmail (1604).

Yet, Nora also shows her facility for Being-Love in this scene as well, offering the first suggestion that she is capable of greater awareness and self-actualization than has been previously demonstrated by her actions thus far in the play. When Rank confesses to Nora that his affections for her could rival Torvald's, that his "body and soul are at [her] command," Nora is unable to press him into service: "I don't need any help. You'll see—it's only my fantasies. That's what it is. Of course!" (Ibsen 1604). Likewise, Nora obliquely confesses her own feelings for Rank to him, feelings that are beyond friendship or the mere desire to exchange affections. "There are some people that one loves most and other people that one would almost prefer being with," she tells him (1605). To clarify, Nora explains that Torvald, like her father, must be the one she "loves most," but when she lived in her father's house, she actually preferred the company of the maids "because they never tried to improve me." Similarly, Dr. Rank symbolizes Nora's ability for Being-Love, one of the conditions of such love being the capacity to "love and accept a person's failing and foibles rather than trying to change them" (Krapp 310). With Dr. Rank, Nora exchanges this deeper form of love, indicating for the first time in the play, what Brian Johnston calls "the evolutionary process whereby the 'mini-Nora' of the opening scenes becomes the 'super-Nora' of the close" (137).

Ironically, this "super-Nora" emerges not when the threats to her safety, love, belonging, and esteem are removed, but, rather, when Nora's fears come to pass. When her husband opens Krogstad's letter, thereby revealing her actions, he reacts with great anger; the "miraculous event" that Nora yearns for, whereby Torvald would "step forward" to take the blame, never materializes. Instead, he worries only about his reputation and social standing, his own need for society's approval and esteem. Nora, however, in having her worst fears materialize, is freed from them. Realizing that they have only been play-acting the perfect marriage, Nora changes, symbolically, out of her dance/performance costume and into her departure clothes, and prepares to leave Torvald. She tells him in what is perhaps the play's most well known scene:

> I went from Papa's hands into yours. You arranged everything to your own taste, and so I got the same taste as you—or pretended to; I can't remember. I guess a little of both, first one, then the other. Now when I look back, it seems as if I'd lived here like a beggar—just from hand to mouth. I've lived by doing tricks for you, Torvald. But that's the way you wanted it. It's a great sin what you and Papa did to me. You're to blame that nothing's become of me. . . . I've been your doll-wife here, just as at home I was Papa's doll-child" (Ibsen 1623).

This key scene, where Nora confronts Torvald and emancipates herself from their child-like play-marriage, still holds great social currency as a feminist manifesto, leading to the play's resurgence in popularity during the 1960s and early 1970s the feminist movement in the United States began what scholars call a second wave. Nora, in leaving behind a marriage in which she is not an equal but a "doll-child," rejects her secondary status in society. "I'm a human being, no less than you" (1624), she tells Torvald. The scene, too, also reveals Nora's growing desire to move beyond the initial stages of identity, into Maslow's highest realm: self-actualization.

Self-actualization, as Maslow described it, involves "the need to fulfill one's potential, to be what one *can* be" (Krapp 311). Here, too, Nora demonstrates this yearning for self-actualization, in her desire for education, for time to "think over these things for [her]self" (Ibsen 1624), even at the expense of lower needs such as safety, belonging, and social esteem. Maslow argues that a person moving toward self-actualization would be "often less restricted by cultural norms and social expectations" than others not operating at this level, and this appears to be true for Nora, who rejects Torvald's attempts to keep her through shaming her, cajoling her, even forbidding her departure and declaring her sick with fever (Krapp 311). For Torvald, who is still operating at the level of esteem, social standing is everything. "Abandon your home, your husband, your children! And you're not even thinking what people will say," he tells her (1624). Nora, however, feels a different calling, one less concerned with social norms than with exploring her true identity: "I can't be concerned about that. I only know how essential this is [...] I have other duties equally sacred [...] duties to myself" (1624). For Nora to achieve self-actualization, she must leave behind Torvald, who desires only her willingness to engage with him at the Deprivation-Love level upon which they have built their marriage. As Sandra Saari contends, "At the end of Act 3, Nora has rationally thought herself into freedom from Torvald's interpretation of reality. She then sets out to define reality for herself" (Saari 1994).

Krogstad, Nora's mirror, also seems to move beyond his initial fears for his security and esteem in rekindling his "Being-Love" with Kristine. In another gesture read as a feminist aspect of the play, Kristine proposes to Krogstad that they unite, if not in marriage, then, at least, in forming a union that allows them, "two shipwrecked people," to "reach across to each other" (Ibsen 1613). Errol Durbach writes that this moment, when "[Kristine] offers Krogstad not sacrifice, but alliance, a life of mutual support, a joining of forces in which individual need is not subordinated to social or sexual expectations, and where strength derives from channeling energy and work into a common enterprise," is "Krogstad's Metamorphosis" (85). It stands in direct contrast to the Helmers' own version of marriage. Like Nora, in the final scene, Krogstad is moved to find an identity beyond financial security and social standing. He is now more concerned with personal happiness and self-fulfillment.

Throughout the play Kristine serves as a foil to Nora and Krogstad, demonstrating a path away from Maslow's lower needs or drives and onward toward a self-created, self-actualized space where one need not compromise one's identity and self. Of all the characters, Kristine has had the greatest difficulty in satisfying her physiological and safety needs, yet she is also, paradoxically, the character least motivated by these drives. Like Nora at the play's conclusion, Kristine is free of their hold on her. Referring to her first marriage, in which she agreed to forfeit her Being-Love for Krogstad and her personal happiness for her deceased husband's ability to provide for her family's physiological and safety needs, Kristine tells Krogstad that "anyone who's sold herself for somebody else once isn't going to do it again" (Ibsen 1614). For these reasons, it is obvious why Nora's first stop in her journey to self-actualization begins by spending the night at Kristine's rather than staying in the doll's house she has built with Torvald.

Neither Krogstad's nor Nora's self-actualization is performed onstage for the audience; instead, we are left at the curtain's closing with Torvald contemplating "the greatest miracle" that can only be possible when characters "transform" themselves (Ibsen 1626). This quest for personal identity takes place beyond the stage, beyond our view, outside the realm of society, for self-actualization is an internal manifestation rather than an externally moti-vated drive. Like Maslow, who believed that an important characteristic of self-actualization was the ability to experience and to recognize "peak experi-ences," so, too, do Ibsen's characters throughout his plays find themselves in "growth promoting" situations that allow them "to look at [their] live[s] in new ways and to find new meaning in life" (Krapp 311). The characters in *A Doll's House* are no exception to this, offering viewers what Durbach calls "a myth of transformation" whereby Nora leaves behind her childhood identity in order to embrace an independent, self-actualized, autonomous one (133). Whether labeled humanist or feminist, this transformation is perhaps why Ibsen's play still feels so contemporary, why *A Doll's House* is still so studied and so often performed today.

Works Cited

Bentley, Eric. "Ibsen: Pro and Con." *Henrik Ibsen*. Ed. Harold Bloom. Philadelphia: Chelsea House, 1999. 25–36.

Durbach, Errol. *A Doll's House: Ibsen's Myth of Transformation*. Boston: Twayne Publishers, 1991.

hooks, bell. *Feminist Theory: From Margin to Center*. Boston: South End Press, 1984.

Ibsen, Henrik. *A Doll's House*. 1879. Trans. Rolf Fjelde. *Literature and Its Writers*, 2nd edition. Eds. Ann Charters and Samuel Charters. Boston and New York: Bedford/St Martin's, 2001. 1575–1627.

Johnston, Brian. *Text and Supertext in Ibsen's Drama*. University Park: Pennsylvania State University Press, 1989.

Krapp, Kristine, ed. "Maslow, Abraham H." *Psychologists and Their Theories for Students*, Vol. 2. Detroit: Gale, 2005. 303–324.

Richardson, Angelique. *The New Woman in Fiction and in Fact: Fin de Siecle Feminisms*. New York: Palgrave Macmillan, 2001.

Saari, Sandra. "Female Becomes Human: Nora Transformed in *A Doll's House*. *Literature and Its Writers*, 2nd edition. Eds. Ann Charters and Samuel Charters. Boston and New York: Bedford/St Martin's, 2001. 1993–1994.

Templeton, Joan. *Ibsen's Women*. Cambridge: Cambridge University Press, 1997.

TERRANCE MCCONNELL

Moral Combat in An Enemy of the People: *Public Health Versus Private Interests*

Introduction

Henrik Ibsen's play, *An Enemy of the People* (1882),[1] is set in the nineteenth century in a Norwegian coastal town. The town has recently opened its Baths, a kind of health resort designed to attract 'visitors' and 'convalescents'. The Baths are expected to bring great economic benefits to the town and enable its citizens to flourish in ways they have not previously.

The protagonist of the play is Thomas Stockmann, a physician. His brother, Peter Stockmann, is the town's mayor. Thomas and Peter have an intense sibling rivalry, a force that is present throughout the play. Early in the play (Act I, p. 6) readers learn that they often quibble about whose idea the Baths were.

Though all of the townspeople are excited about what the Baths will do for their standard of living, early on readers are alerted that Dr Stockmann may have uncovered a problem (Act I, pp. 10–11). Because some of the previous patrons had become more ill, Dr Stockmann had taken a sample of the water and requested that a local university test it. The results are back. Dr Stockmann declares that the Baths are a 'cesspool', 'poisoned' and a 'serious danger to health' (Act I, p. 18). The pipes must be re-laid in order to purify the water. Though this will be inconvenient, Dr Stockmann expects to be treated as a hero (Act I, pp. 19–20).

From *Public Health Ethics* 3, no. 1 (April 2010): 80–86. Copyright © 2010 Terrance McConnell.

Dr Stockmann's expectations prove to be naïve, however. The press—represented by Hovstad, editor of the *People's Herald*, Billing, a journalist, and Aslaksen, a printer—claim that they will give Dr Stockmann full support. When Mayor Stockmann questions the report's accuracy and points out how costly it will be to re-lay the pipes, however, the press's allegiance changes. Dr Stockmann becomes an object of ridicule and is eventually declared 'an enemy of the people' (Act IV, p. 85).

Given how quickly the press and the townspeople turn against Dr Stockmann, and given that they do so based on little or no evidence, one suspects that this play is a critique of one aspect of democracy. Arthur Miller suggests that a central theme of the play 'is the question of whether the democratic guarantees protecting political minorities ought to be set aside in times of crises' (Miller (1950): 8). This seems correct, and such a theme gives the play much contemporary interest. But there is another theme at work that is also of consequence to contemporary readers. The three main characters in this play—Thomas Stockmann, Peter Stockmann and Thomas's wife, Katherine—each has special obligations in virtue of his or her role. But these special obligations are not jointly dischargeable. The moral success of one agent seems to require the moral failure of another. These agents are in what Heidi Hurd calls 'moral combat' (Hurd, 1999).[2] Dr Stockmann's role as a physician gives him a special obligation to look out for the health of people. But correcting the problem with the Baths may have an adverse effect on his community. Such a conflict may be similar to those faced by other physicians who occupy dual roles, such as those asked to assist the state in carrying out the death penalty, or by doctors who are serving in the military.

The Interests of the Town

Thomas Stockmann believes that exposure to the Baths will harm patrons and it is wrong to do so. No special obligations are needed to endorse this position. But he is also a physician committed to promoting the health of people. As such, he is apt to feel a strong obligation to the patrons, even if he is not the cause of the harm. Thomas is also a member of the board governing the Baths. So he might reasonably think that he is doubly responsible were he to lure people into a situation that will cause them harm. No doubt there is a general obligation—one borne by all moral agents—not to harm others. But it is easy to see why Thomas Stockmann also feels the force of special obligations to those who might become ill as a result of using the Baths. Indeed, the town is making a pitch to those who are sick to use these facilities.

As mayor, Peter Stockmann has an obligation to do what is best for the town. Even if all citizens of the town have such an obligation, Peter has a special moral requirement that goes beyond those of the others. It is not surprising, then, that even before he learns about the specific nature of the problem, Peter insists that Thomas and all others subordinate themselves 'to the authorities charged with the welfare of that community' (Act I, p. 10). This immediately tilts the debate Peter's way; the standard to be used is the welfare of the town.

Thomas Stockmann shared the report detailing the Baths' pollution with Peter. Having read the report, Peter marshals multiple arguments against shutting down the Baths and re-laying the pipes. His first argument appeals to the citizens' economic interests. The town is currently prospering and there is every reason to believe that it will continue doing so. If the Baths are closed, the principal source of income for the town will be shut off. And if the pipes must be re-laid, that will be costly (Act II, pp. 34–35). The Mayor later supplements this argument by pointing out to Hovstad and Aslaksen that the costs of re-laying the pipes will fall on townspeople in the form of higher taxes. So both the town as a whole and individual citizens in particular will be worse off if Dr Stockmann's solution is adopted.

Even though the Mayor may have self-interested reasons for suppressing the report, we can concede that he wants to do what is in the best interests of the town and that he believes that shutting down the Baths is contrary to those interests. In order to prevail, the Mayor needs for others to see the issue in this way. So he tells Thomas that this matter is not just a scientific one; instead, 'it is a combination of technical and economic factors' (Act II, p. 39). The strategy here is to disarm Dr Stockmann by removing the issue from his area of expertise. This approach need not be seen as totally disingenuous. Earlier Hovstad had warned Thomas that things might be more complicated than he realized; 'it probably hasn't struck you that it's tied up with a lot of other things' (Act II, p. 25). It is certainly true that closing the Baths will have an impact on the welfare of the townspeople.

Peter's second argument may be disingenuous. He says, 'I am not entirely convinced by your report that the state of the Baths is as serious as you make out' (Act II, p. 35). This, in effect, denies that there is a problem, or at least a serious one. Contemporary readers might expect the Mayor to say that the report is based on 'junk science'. There are two reasons to suspect Peter of duplicity here. First, whether the Baths are polluted is a scientific matter, and Peter is not an expert in this area nor has he cited reports of experts. Peter seems to be doing nothing more than denying what is for him an inconvenient truth. Second, the Mayor later proposes a solution of his own. But a solution is not needed unless there is a real problem.

Peter advances a third argument, one that appeals to Thomas's obligations as a member of the governing board of the Baths. The Mayor is the head of this board, and so he is the final authority about all that it does. He says,

'But as a subordinate member of the staff of the Baths, you have no right to express any opinion that conflicts with that of your superiors' (Act II, p. 39). Earlier, even before he was aware of the nature of the problem, Peter had expressed the same principle: 'The individual must be ready to subordinate himself ... to the authorities charged with the welfare of that community' (Act I, p. 10). This argument, if correct, does not establish substantively what ought to be done regarding the Baths; instead, it shows who ought to make the decision.

Peter alludes to a fourth argument, though it is not fully developed. In this case, he appeals to Thomas's obligations to his own family. 'Did you never think what consequences this might have for you personally?' 'For you and your family' (Act II, p. 37). And later, he adds, 'Try to realize what you owe to yourself and family' (Act II, p. 41). This can be perceived either as a mere threat or as a moral argument. Seen as the former, the Mayor is simply warning Thomas that he will lose his job if he tells the public about the alleged problem. Viewed as the latter, Peter is reminding his brother that he has obligations as a husband and a father, and his ability to carry out those obligations will be compromised if he follows through with his plan.

If Mayor Stockmann is a sincere moral combatant, he believes that he ought to do whatever is necessary for the community's best interests. Convincing Thomas not to announce to the public that the Baths are tainted is therefore necessary. Peter's second argument denies that there is such a problem. His first argument—the one that is most honest—asks Thomas to look at the welfare of all potentially affected parties. If he goes public, people in his own town will be harmed. The issue is economic as well as technical. When the overall calculations are done, the Mayor's proposal will be best for all. The third argument is procedural rather than substantive—Dr Stockmann has no right to speak publicly about this issue. And the fourth argument urges Thomas to focus on another of his roles, that of husband and father. This kind of 'shotgun' approach makes sense when we consider that Peter believes that as a moral combatant he must prevail.

So what does Peter recommend? First: 'It will therefore be necessary for you to make a public denial of these rumours' (Act II, p. 38). This is designed to keep the Baths open and thus preserve the town's economic interests. But what about the interests of future patrons? 'The existing water-supply for the Baths is now an established fact, and must be treated as such. But it is reasonable to suppose that ... it would be possible to initiate certain improvements' (Act II, p. 35). The Mayor can thus say that his proposal looks out for the welfare of all. If the rumors can be squashed, the town will continue to flourish economically. If appropriate improvements are gradually introduced, the Baths eventually will be safe for all. It is true that in the short term some patrons may be harmed; but the best outcome for all is the gradualist approach. The fewest people will be harmed the least if this is done.

Familial Obligations

Peter is not Thomas's only moral opponent. His wife, Katherine, also has a moral stake in the situation. Katherine sees clearly that Thomas is likely to lose his job and she knows what that will do to the welfare of their children. Katherine points out that if Thomas continues his fight with Peter, he will probably lose his job. Thomas retorts that 'at least I shall have done my duty by the public . . . and by society'. Katherine makes the obvious reply: 'But what about your family, Thomas? What about us at home? Will you be doing your duty by the ones you should provide for first?' (Act II, p. 42)

Mrs Stockmann believes that she has an obligation to promote the welfare of her children, and that Dr Stockmann is bound by this same requirement. She need not believe that these are their only moral requirements, though in the passage quoted she implies that their duties to the children trump all others. What she suggests to Thomas is that his first duty is to provide for his family. If she convinces him of this, it will enable her to discharge her duties that are imperiled by the moral combat. But readers need not doubt her sincerity here. We may presume that she believes that Thomas's first duty too is to his family.

Katherine advances two other arguments, more pragmatic in nature, designed to convince Thomas to comply with Peter's request. She says that Peter, as Mayor, is far more politically powerful than Thomas. The doctor replies that he has right on his side. Katherine's response: 'Right! Yes, of course. But what's the use of right without might?' (Act II, p. 41) The point of this argument is that even if Thomas's position is morally the best, he is likely not to prevail. Thus, he will exert energy and sacrifice his own interests, and still fail to achieve the desired end. This seems to render his sacrifices fruitless.

Katherine's other pragmatic argument is a critique of Thomas's idealism. When Thomas complains that he has been treated unjustly by Peter, Hovstad, Billing and Aslaksen, Katherine agrees. 'Yes, they've treated you disgracefully, I will say that. But heavens! Once you start thinking of all the injustices in this world people have to put up with . . .' (Act II, p. 43). Katherine is making the familiar point that one must pick one's battles. Fighting all injustices in the world is not possible. The rational person will determine where his efforts will make a difference and direct his energies there. But, as Katherine has already argued, Thomas is not going to prevail against Peter. So in terms of making a positive impact on the world, Thomas should give up this fight and devote himself to more feasible causes. If he agrees to this, that will enable him and Katherine to do what is best for their children.

So, according to Katherine, it is foreseeable that Thomas's struggle to have the Baths closed and the pipes re-laid will fail. In addition, this fight will cost Thomas his job and his standing in the town. Though I earlier characterized Katherine's latter two arguments as 'pragmatic', that may not be accurate. For she may be appealing to the principle that 'ought' implies 'can'. If it is not within Thomas's power to bring it about that the Baths are closed until the problem is corrected, he is not obligated to do so. But if he continues to pursue this course in vain, the consequences for his family will be horrible. So understood, Katherine is portraying Thomas's idealism as not only naïve but also unethical.[3]

There are similarities in the positions of Peter and Katherine. Each appeals to a role that Thomas occupies and argues that there are important obligations attached to that role. The Mayor reminds Thomas that he is a citizen and as such has an obligation to do what is best for the town; or, more properly, to obey those who have the authority to determine what is best for the town. Revealing the alleged problems with the Baths is contrary to the town's interests, and so is forbidden. Katherine insists that parents have an obligation to do what is best for their children, and if Thomas defies Peter he will render himself unable to discharge that requirement. Peter and Katherine each points to consequences that will ensue if Thomas does what he threatens, but each focuses on the consequences for a different population.

Thomas Stockmann is not persuaded by either his brother or his wife. But in rejecting their arguments, does he reject the role-related morality to which they appeal? The answer to this is complicated.

First, Do No Harm

We can imagine at least four different answers that Dr Stockmann might give to the arguments just explained. He might agree with Peter that he ought to be a good citizen, but claim that releasing the report and correcting the problem is exactly what a good citizen should do. He might agree with Katherine that he ought to be a good parent, but assert that being honest and living according to one's principles is what a good parent should do. Yet a third response is to claim that his obligations as doctor require him to protect the health of would-be patrons, and that in this situation these obligations take precedence over his obligations as a citizen and as a parent. Finally, he might argue that role-related obligations either are irrelevant or do not prevail here. There is a general obligation—one borne by all moral agents—not to cause harm to others. That obligation will be violated unless the problem with the Baths is corrected. There is some evidence that Thomas makes all of these points in defending his position. This suggests that he believes that his various role-related obligations are in harmony.

During one of the disputes with Peter, Thomas says, 'I'm the one with the real welfare of the town at heart. All I want to do is expose certain things that are bound to come out sooner or later anyway' (Act II, p. 40). If the Baths are polluted, as the report shows, then eventually enough patrons will become ill and people will realize the source of the problem. That will be worse, in the long run, for the town's interests than if they acknowledge the problem and deal with it. Losses will occur either way; but a policy of honesty will minimize those losses. Here Thomas is accusing Peter of being naïve. The gradualist approach of correcting the problem before patrons discover it is bound to fail.

When, at the end of Act II, Katherine pleads with Thomas to focus on what is best for his children, he says, 'I want to be able to look my boys in the face when they grow up into free men' (Act II, p. 43). The suggestion here is that one cannot be a good parent unless one exhibits moral integrity. To do that, agents must abide by their principles. If Thomas were to give up this fight, he would be setting a bad example for his children. Toward the end of the play, when Petra, his daughter, has lost her job, when his sons, Morten and Ejlif, have been permanently dismissed from school, and when his family has been evicted from their home, Thomas says to the boys, 'I'll make decent and independent-minded men of you both' (Act V, p. 105). Readers need not assume here that Dr Stockmann is completely oblivious to the basic needs of his family. Indeed, he says to the entire family, 'Well, you'll just have to skimp and scrape a bit on the side—we'll manage all right. That's my least worry' (Act V, p. 104). Even if with regard to these necessities the children are not as well off as previously, their basic needs will be fulfilled and their moral development will have been advanced.

Contemporary readers might expect Thomas to emphasize his obligations as a physician; but there is comparatively little of that in the text. In one exchange, however, the issue seems to arise. In a discussion with Hovstad, Billing and Katherine, Thomas points out that the Baths are being commended 'for the sick'. This tells us that the town is promoting the Baths as a panacea for various illnesses. Yet Thomas has observed over the past year 'a number of curious cases of sickness among the visitors'. Based on this and the report, he concludes that the Baths are 'extremely dangerous to health' (Act I, pp. 17, 18 and 19). While there are several ways to understand this exchange, one natural reading is this. As a physician, Thomas has a special obligation to protect and promote the health of people. The Baths are being advertised as helpful for the sick. Yet Thomas believes that they actually cause illness. So he has a special obligation to intervene in order to protect the health of potential patrons. Moreover, as a member of the board, he will be complicit in the harm that ensues.

All of these responses work within the framework of role-related morality. Dr Stockmann tries to convince interlocutors that releasing the report to the public and correcting the problem with the Baths are obligations supported by their relevant roles. But it seems plausible to think that role-related obligations are not the key to Thomas's position. Instead, he seems to hold that all agents ought to be honest and to prevent harm when they can. Recall that the Mayor proposed that Thomas publicly deny that there were any problems with the Baths. If Thomas would do this, then Peter would implement his gradualist approach and 'take some suitable precautionary measures and treat any noticeable injurious effects'. Thomas has a rather sharp description of Peter's proposal: 'A swindle, a fraud, an absolute crime against the public and against society!' (Act II, p. 35) It is wrong to deceive people, wrong to lure the sick to the Baths, and wrong to put others in harm's way, regardless of one's role in society. Later, toward the end, Thomas tells Katherine that one of his motives is to show 'that policies of expediency are turning all our standards of morality and justice upside down, so that life's just not going to be worth living' (Act V, p. 104). Thomas thinks that there is something rotten in the town—that it, like the Baths, is polluted—and that a morality of expediency is one source of the corruption. Sometimes individuals and even whole societies must sacrifice their own interests in order to do what is right.

An ethics of expediency, as Thomas understands it, is one that calculates the impact of policies on various parties and then chooses policies based on which has the most favorable impact on a selected group. For Peter, that group is the townspeople; for Katherine, her family. In rejecting an ethics of expediency, Thomas is saying that it is wrong to promote the welfare of some at the direct expense of others.

How are we to evaluate Thomas's position?

Contra Expediency

One of Thomas's replies to Peter initially seems plausible. Thomas says that the problem will eventually be revealed, and so fixing it now is the least costly solution. Today, with information flow as rapid as it is, we readers are apt to nod in agreement. But perhaps we should examine this closer. Three factors suggest that Peter's deceitful gradualist approach may be one that he can pull off. First, in this town at this time, the exchange of information will be slow. Second, many who use the Baths will already be ill. So the fact that they become sicker will not be a surprise and so will not be immediately attributed to the Baths. Third, the patrons are mostly visitors. So after using the Baths, they will scatter about the country, and even the Continent. Even if many of them experience problems after using the Baths, it will likely take a long time to see the common link. There is no one individual or group who will have enough information to draw the pertinent conclusion. We have seen this often throughout history. The problem with thalidomide in the 1950s is one such example. So working within Peter's own 'ethics of expediency' may not be Thomas's best strategy.

What about the argument with Katherine? Her prediction that Thomas could not prevail in a political battle with Peter proved correct. Not only did Thomas lose his job, but Petra lost her teaching position, the boys were dismissed from school, and the entire family was evicted from the house they were renting. Even in the nineteenth century, whistleblowers did not fare well. But for an offer from Captain Horster (Act V, p. 103)—a man who is apolitical but suspicious of majorities—to stay with him, the family would have been homeless. The bigger question, however, is which interests of the children Thomas and Katherine should be promoting. With respect to basic necessities—food, shelter and education—there can be little doubt that the Stockmann children are worse off at the play's end than before their father was declared 'an enemy of the people'. But if the children have additional interests and if their economic interests do not fall below what is acceptable, then perhaps Thomas is right. He believes that his children's moral development and moral education are seriously compromised if he accedes to Peter's ethics of expediency. Thomas's position need not assume that economic interests and moral interests are commensurable. He may instead hold that as long as the children are well off enough with respect to economic interests, then good parents will promote other interests as well. If this is his view, then it suggests that he thinks that the familiar 'best interests' principle is too simple. Katherine did eventually switch sides: 'I'll stick by you, Thomas!' (Act III, p. 65) It is not clear, however, if this is because she is morally persuaded by his argument or if she is merely playing the role of a supportive wife.

Even if Thomas converted Katherine by 'playing on her turf'—appealing to the interests of the children—a comparable strategy will not work in his dispute with Peter. The Mayor will not be convinced that it is in the town's interests or in his own interests to tell the public about the problem with the Baths. Here Thomas must reject the ethics of expediency. And so he does. His first reaction is that it is wrong to harm others knowingly; to do so is a violation of their rights. After Dr Stockmann explains to the newspaper men that the Baths are 'dangerous to health', Hovstad asks him what he is going to do. He replies, 'To see the matter put right, of course.' (Act I, p. 19)

There is no hesitation on his part and no calculation of the impact on the interests of the townspeople.

There is another way to put Thomas's position. It is simply morally inappropriate to compare the loss of benefits for the town with the harm done to the patrons, as does Peter's ethics of expediency. If the Baths remain open, the patrons are being harmed; if the Baths are temporarily closed, the townspeople are being denied a benefit. The losses of the two parties are on a different moral plane. The obligation not to harm takes priority over the obligation to provide benefits, even if one has a role-related obligation to provide for the welfare of the town. When Peter urges Thomas to think about the losses that the townspeople will incur if the Baths are closed, Thomas's reply is straightforward: 'We live by peddling filth and corruption! The whole of the town's prosperity is rooted in a lie.' (Act II, p.41) The core mistake in the Mayor's position is that loss of benefit is morally equivalent with harm and that these must be weighed each against the other. Thomas denies this. Prosperity that is rooted in the deliberate infliction of harm compromises the integrity of those who are prospering. Thomas's response anticipates Bernard Williams' criticism of utilitarianism nearly a century later (Williams (1973): 108–118).

Lessons Learned

Peter's two-pronged attack in response to the problem raised by the report should be familiar to contemporary readers. One prong—the ethics of expediency—appeals to the overall interests of all affected parties. The economic interests of the townspeople are on a par with and are to be weighed against the harm that will come to future patrons of the Baths. Moreover, if the problem is corrected, not only will the townspeople be denied the income from the Baths, but they will also have to pay for the repairs in the form of additional taxes. This is ingeniously designed to convince people that the overall good happens to coincide with what is best for them.

The second prong of Peter's attack is to deny that there is a serious problem. Minor tinkering will make the Baths safe. This is a common strategy. For years cigarette companies played the role of the skeptic by challenging claims that their product had a negative impact on the health of its users. And the campaign to convince the public that global warming is a hoax is legendary.[4] This second prong is important. The public, represented by those from the *People's Herald*, is not willing to side with Peter until he raises doubts about the report's veracity. It seems to say something good about people that they are not willing to approve of a policy or action when it benefits them at the expense of the welfare of others. On the other hand, it is disappointing that they are so easily convinced that what they are doing is not really harmful to others. Hovstad, Billing and Aslaksen were convinced that the report about the Baths was false merely because Peter said that it was; he offered no evidence.

Thomas, too, delivered a multipronged attack. He *argued* that acknowledging the problem and repairing the Baths was in the best interests of the town, and that his action of exposing the problem was best for his family because it taught the children not to abandon their principles. His core position, however, was that knowingly exposing people to harm is wrong, even if doing so would reap profits for the town. As a moral combatant, it was important to Thomas to win. For winning would mean that the public had been alerted to the Baths' contamination, and thereby had their health and rights protected. Thomas need not deny that the interests of the town and the interests of his children are important. But these interests may not be advanced by harming others.

In one sense, Thomas is an idealist urging others to sacrifice at least their short-term interests in order to do what is right. One message of the play is that those with vested interests will try to silence the idealist. When the *People's Herald* refuses to print Thomas's article about the problem with the Baths, he calls a meeting of the townspeople. His plan is to explain the problems to them in a speech. But Peter prevents him from speaking by appealing to fear. The version of Peter's argument in Arthur Miller's adaptation of *An Enemy of the People* is powerful. '[I]n ordinary times I'd agree a hundred per cent with anybody's right to say anything. But these are not ordinary times. Nations have crises, and so do towns' (Miller (1950): 89). Peter goes on:

> Now this is our crisis . . . Today we're just on the verge of becoming internationally known as a resort. I predict that within five years the income of every man in this room will be immensely greater. . . . I predict that if we are not defamed and maliciously attacked we will someday be one of the richest and most beautiful resort towns in the world. (Miller (1950): 90)[5]

'Crisis ethics' is one tool that is used to silence idealists.

A second message in the play concerns how the idealist is portrayed by others. When Thomas tells Peter that he will proclaim the truth about the Baths on every street corner, the Mayor calls him 'absolutely crazy' (Act III, p. 65). When Morten Kiil tries to force Dr Stockmann to recant by tying all of Katherine's inheritance to stocks in the Baths, Thomas nevertheless refuses. This prompts Kiil to say, 'But you couldn't be so stark, staring mad as all that, not when it affects your wife and children' (Act V, p. 97). When Hovstad threatens to accuse Dr Stockmann of conspiring with Kiil to drive down the cost of stock in the Baths so that they could gain a monopoly, again he will not budge. This prompts Hovstad to ask, 'Have you gone completely mad?' (Act V, p. 101) All of this is designed to marginalize Thomas. At the play's end, after the Stockmanns have lost most of their worldly possessions, Thomas declares, 'I'm one of the strongest men in the whole world' (Act V, p. 105). Does he not recognize how utterly ineffective he has been? But Thomas is not insane for he goes on to explain what he means: 'The thing is, you see, that the strongest man in the world is the man who stands alone' (Act V, p. 106). He is asserting that agents should not abandon their principles even if there is a price to pay, as long as the family's basic needs are met.

One conclusion that might be reached after reading this text is that the role-related obligations of politicians to their constituents and of parents to their children are limited by the rights of others. Whenever what is best for one's constituents or what is best for one's children involves putting innocent third parties at risk, one may not pursue the best for those individuals. As long as the options remaining are 'good enough'—meet the basic needs of the constituents or the children—then situations of moral combat may be limited, though not necessarily eliminated completely.

Notes

1. Henrik Ibsen, *An Enemy of the People* (New York: Oxford University Press, 1960). 'Introduction', 'Select Bibliography' and 'Chronology of Henrik Ibsen' by James McFarlane. Page references will be given parenthetically in the text.

2. Elsewhere this same phenomenon has been dubbed 'interpersonal moral conflicts.' See McConnell (1988).

3. The need to make this clarification of Katherine's position was pointed out to me by both David Lefkowitz and Sandra Shapshay.

4. For a recent account of the role that scientists have played in such campaigns, see Michaels (2008).

5. In Miller's adaptation, this occurs in Act II, Scene 2; in Ibsen's play, the comparable speech is in Act IV (pp. 70–71).

References

Hurd H. *Moral Combat.* New York: Cambridge University Press; 1999.

Ibsen H. *An Enemy of the People.* New York: Oxford University Press; 1960/1882. ["Introduction," "Select Bibliography," and "Chronology of Henrik Ibsen" by Mcfarlane, J.]

McConnell T. Interpersonal Moral Conflicts. *American Philosophical Quarterly.* 1988;25:25–35.

Michaels D. *Doubt Is Their Product: How Industry's Assault on Science Threatens Your Health.* New York: Oxford University Press; 2008.

Miller A. *Adaptation of An Enemy of the People.* New York: Penguin Books; 1950.

Chronology

1828	Born in Skien, Norway, on March 20, to Marichen and Knud Ibsen, a merchant.
1834–35	Father's business fails and the family moves to Venstoep, a town a few miles outside of Skien.
1844	Becomes assistant to an apothecary in the seaport town of Grimstad.
1846	Illegitimate son born to Else Sofie Jensdatter.
1849	Writes first play, *Catiline*.
1850	Enters the university in Christiana, now the city of Oslo, and writes second play, *The Warrior's Barrow*.
1851	Joins newly formed National Theater in Bergen, where he will stay for the next six years.
1852	Writes *St. John's Eve*, a romantic comedy.
1853	*St. John's Eve* is performed in Bergen but fails.
1854	Writes *Lady Inger of Oestraat*, a historical tragedy.
1855	*Lady Inger of Oestraat* is performed at Bergen and also fails. Writes the romantic comedy *The Feast at Solhaug*.
1856	*The Feast at Solhaug* is performed at Bergen, which garners a small measure of success. Writes *Olaf Liljekrans*.

1857	*Olaf Liljekrans* is performed at Bergen. It is not a success. Writes *The Vikings at Helgeland*.
1858	Marries Suzannah Thoreson. *The Vikings at Helgeland* is staged and is a small success.
1859	A son, Sigurd, is born.
1860–61	Suffers poverty and despair and is unable to write.
1862	Writes *Love's Comedy*. The National Theatre in Bergen goes bankrupt. Awarded university grant to gather Norwegian folk songs and tales.
1863	Takes part-time job as literary adviser to the Danish-controlled Christiania Theatre. Writes *The Pretenders* and is granted a government stipend.
1864	*The Pretenders* is staged at the Christiania Theatre and is a success. Moves to Rome, and remains abroad for the next twenty-seven years.
1865	Writes *Brand*.
1866	*Brand* published to critical acclaim, bringing Ibsen fame throughout Scandinavia.
1867	Writes *Peer Gynt*. Its publication garners even greater praise than *Brand* and increases Ibsen's recognition as a playwright.
1868	Moves to Dresden.
1869	Completes *The League of Youth*.
1871	Publishes a volume of poetry, *Poems*.
1873	Completes *Emperor and Galilean*, begun nine years prior.
1874	Moves to Munich.
1877	Completes *The Pillars of Society*.
1878	Returns to Italy for a year.
1879	Writes *A Doll's House*. Returns to Munich for a year.
1880	Moves to Italy.
1881	Writes *Ghosts*. The play is rejected by theaters and publishers in response to public outrage against its exploration of free love and venereal disease.

1882	Writes *An Enemy of the People*. *Ghosts* is performed in the United States.
1884	Writes *The Wild Duck*.
1885	Returns to Munich and visits Norway for the first time since 1874.
1886	Writes *Rosmersholm*.
1888	Writes *The Lady from the Sea*.
1890	Writes *Hedda Gabler*.
1891	Resettles permanently in Norway.
1892	Writes *The Master Builder*.
1894	Writes *Little Eyolf*.
1896	Writes *John Gabriel Borkman*.
1898	First volumes of collected works published in Copenhagen.
1899	Writes *When We Dead Awaken*.
1901	Suffers a stroke and is partially paralyzed.
1903	Second stroke leaves him helpless and dependent.
1906	Dies in Christiania, Norway, on May 23, at the age of 78

Contributors

HAROLD BLOOM is Sterling Professor of the Humanities at Yale University. Educated at Cornell and Yale universities, he is the author of more than 30 books, including *Shelley's Mythmaking* (1959), *The Visionary Company* (1961), *Blake's Apocalypse* (1963), *Yeats* (1970), *The Anxiety of Influence* (1973), *A Map of Misreading* (1975), *Kabbalah and Criticism* (1975), *Agon: Toward a Theory of Revisionism* (1982), *The American Religion* (1992), *The Western Canon* (1994), *Omens of Millennium: The Gnosis of Angels, Dreams, and Resurrection* (1996), *Shakespeare: The Invention of the Human* (1998), *How to Read and Why* (2000), *Genius: A Mosaic of One Hundred Exemplary Creative Minds* (2002), *Hamlet: Poem Unlimited* (2003), *Where Shall Wisdom Be Found?* (2004), and *Jesus and Yahweh: The Names Divine* (2005). In addition, he is the author of hundreds of articles, reviews, and editorial introductions. In 1999, Professor Bloom received the American Academy of Arts and Letters' Gold Medal for Criticism. He has also received the International Prize of Catalonia, the Alfonso Reyes Prize of Mexico, and the Hans Christian Andersen Bicentennial Prize of Denmark.

EVERT SPRINCHORN is a professor emeritus of Vassar College. He is author of *The Genius of the Scandinavian Theater* and other titles. He is editor and translator *of Ibsen's Letters and Speeches* and coeditor *of The Columbia Encyclopedia of Modern Drama*.

ERROL DURBACH is a retired theater professor of the University of British Columbia. He has adapted and translated Ibsen plays. He is the author of *A Doll's House: Ibsen's Myth of Transformation* and has published other works on Ibsen as well.

JAMES WALTER MCFARLANE was an emeritus professor at the University of East Anglia. He was general editor of the eight-volume *Oxford Ibsen* and the author of several books on Ibsen, among them *Ibsen and Meaning*.

INGA-STINA EWBANK was an emeritus professor at the University of Leeds. She translated several of Ibsen's and Strindberg's plays for the English stage and was the author of many critical works, with special emphasis on Ibsen and Strindberg.

ERIC BENTLEY is an emeritus professor at Columbia University. He has published numerous titles on theater, edited many works of dramatists, translated many titles, and also written his own plays.

TANYA THRESHER is an associate professor of Scandinavian studies at the University of Wisconsin, Madison. She earned a Ph.D. in Scandinavian studies from the University of Washington and an M.A. and B.A. from the University of East Anglia, Norwich, United Kingdom. In addition to articles on Ibsen and contemporary Norwegian dramatists, she has published *Cecilie Løveid: Engendering a Dramatic Tradition* (2005) and was the editor of *A Dictionary of Literary Biography: Twentieth Century Norwegian Writers* (2004).

KRISTIN BRUNNEMER received a Ph.D. from the University of California, Riverside. Her areas of specialization include film and visual culture, media studies, comparative minority discourse, and twentieth-century American literature. She is the author of articles on Ana Castillo, Wanda Coleman, and Maria Weston Fordham.

TERRANCE MCCONNELL is a professor of philosophy at the University of North Carolina at Greensboro. He is the author of *Inalienable Rights: The Limits of Consent in Medicine and the Law, Gratitude,* and *Moral Issues in Health Care.*

Bibliography

Adler, Stella. *Adler on Ibsen, Strindberg, and Chekhov*, edited preface by Barry Paris. New York: Knopf, 1999.

Binding, Paul. *With Vine-Leaves in His Hair: The Role of the Artist in Ibsen's Plays.* Norwich: Norvik Press, 2006.

Brustein, Robert. "The Fate of Ibsenism." *Scandinavian Review* 66, no. 4 (1978): 7–19.

Chamberlain, John S. *Ibsen, the Open Vision.* London: Athlone, 1982.

Demastes, William W. "Re-Inspecting the Crack in the Chimney: Chaos Theory from Ibsen to Stoppard." *New Theatre Quarterly* 10, no. 39 (August 1994): 242–54.

Egan, Michael, ed. *Henrik Ibsen: The Critical Heritage.* London; New York: Routledge, 1997.

Ewbank, Inga-Stina. "Reading Ibsen's Signs: Ambivalence on Page and Stage (Plenary Address)." *Ibsen Studies* 4, no. 1 (2004): 4–17.

———. "'Spiritual Property': Intertextuality and Influence in Ibsen's Texts." *Contemporary Approaches to Ibsen* 9 (1997): 35–50.

Fjelde, Rolf. "The Lady from the Sea: Ibsen's Positive World-View in a Topographic Figure." *Modern Drama* 21 (1978): 379–91.

———. "What Makes a Masterpiece? Ibsen and the Western World." *Modern Drama* 28, no. 4 (December 1985): 581–90.

Foster, Verna A. "Ibsen's Tragicomedy: *The Wild Duck*." *Modern Drama* 38, no. 3 (Fall 1995): 287–97.

Gallagher-Ross, Jacob, ed. "Ibsen Our Contemporary." *Theater* 37, no. 3 (2007): 87–115.

Goldman, Michael. "*When We Dead Awaken*: A Scene That Gets Out of Control." *Modern Drama* 49, no. 3 (Fall 2006): 387–95.

Innes, Christopher, ed. *Sourcebook on Naturalist Theatre*. London; New York: Routledge, 2000.

Jacobsen, Per Schelde, and Barbara Fass Leavy. *Ibsen's Forsaken Merman: Folklore in the Late Plays*. New York: New York University Press, 1988.

Johnsen, William A. "Ibsen's Drama of Self-Sacrifice." *Contagion: Journal of Violence, Mimesis, and Culture* 3 (Spring 1996): 141–61.

———. *Violence and Modernism: Ibsen, Joyce, and Woolf*. Gainesville: University Press of Florida, 2003.

Johnston, Brian. *The Ibsen Cycle: The Design of the Plays from* Pillars of Society *to* When We Dead Awaken. University Park: Pennsylvania State University Press, 1992.

———. "Ibsen's Cycle as Hegelian Tragedy." *Comparative Drama* 33, no. 1 (Spring 1999): 140–65.

Lebowitz, Naomi. *Ibsen and the Great World*. Baton Rouge: Louisiana University Press, 1990.

Ledger, Sally. *Henrik Ibsen*. Plymouth: Northcote House in association with the British Council, 1999.

Manheim, Michael. *Vital Contradictions: Characterization in the Plays of Ibsen, Strindberg, Chekhov and O'Neill*. Brussels, Belgium: Peter Lang, 2002.

Marker, Frederick J., and Christopher Innes, ed. *Modernism in European Drama: Ibsen, Strindberg, Pirandello, Beckett: Essays from Modern Drama*. Toronto; Buffalo: University of Toronto Press, 1998.

May, Keith M. *Ibsen and Shaw*. London: Macmillan, 1985.

McFarlane, James. *Ibsen & Meaning: Studies, Essays & Prefaces 1953–87*. Norwich, England: Norvik, 1989.

Newton, K. M. *Modern Literature and the Tragic*. Edinburgh, Scotland: Edinburgh University Press, 2008.

Olson, Liesl. *Modernism and the Ordinary*. Oxford; New York: Oxford University Press, 2009.

Perridon, Harry, ed. *Strindberg, Ibsen & Bergman: Essays on Scandinavian Film and Drama*. Maastricht: Shaker Publishing, 1998.

Proceedings, International Ibsen Conference: Socio-Political Aspects of Ibsen's Plays, Dhaka, Bangladesh 11–13, May. Dhaka: Centre for Asian Theatre, 2006.

Reynolds, Paige. *Modernism, Drama, and the Audience for Irish Spectacle*. Cambridge, England: Cambridge University Press, 2007.

Rhodes, Norman. *Ibsen and the Greeks: The Classical Greek Dimension in Selected Works of Henrik Ibsen as Mediated by German and Scandinavian Culture*. Lewisburg [Pa.]: Bucknell University Press; London: Associated University Presses, 1995.

Robinson, Michael, ed. *Turning the Century: Centennial Essays on Ibsen*. Norwich: Norvik Press, 2006.

Rokem, Freddie. *Theatrical Space in Ibsen, Chekhov, and Strindberg: Public Forms of Privacy*. Ann Arbor, Mich.: UMI Research Press, 1986.

Rustin, Margaret, and Michael Rustin. *Mirror to Nature: Drama, Psychoanalysis and Society*. London; New York: Karnac, 2002.

Saether, Astrid, ed. *Ibsen, Tragedy, and the Tragic*. Oslo, Norway: Centre for Ibsen Studies, University of Oslo, 2003.

Schanke, Robert A. *Ibsen in America: A Century of Change*. Metuchen, N.J.: Scarecrow Press, 1988.

Templeton, Joan. "Ibsen's Legacy: Making the Theater Matter." *Scandinavian Review* 94, no. 2 (Autumn–Winter 2006): 30–41.

———. *Ibsen's Women*. Cambridge; New York: Cambridge University Press, 1997.

Thomas, David. *Henrik Ibsen*. London: Macmillan, 1983.

Van Laan, Thomas F. "Generic Complexity in Ibsen's *An Enemy of the People*." *Comparative Drama* 20, no. 2 (Summer 1986): 95–114.

———. "Ibsen and Nietzsche." *Scandinavian Studies* 78, no. 3 (Fall 2006): 255–302.

———. "The Tragic Vision of Ibsen's *Rosmersholm*." *Modern Drama* 49, no. 3 (Fall 2006): 370–86.

Weinstein, Arnold. *Northern Arts: The Breakthrough of Scandinavian Literature and Art, from Ibsen to Bergman*. Princeton: Princeton University Press, 2008.

Williams, Raymond. *Modern Tragedy*. Peterborough, ON: Broadview, 2006.

Zeineddine, Nada. *Because It Is My Name: Problems of Identity Experienced by Women, Artists, and Breadwinners in the Plays of Henrik Ibsen, Tennessee Williams, and Arthur Miller*. Braunton, [England]: Merlin, 1991.

Acknowledgments

Evert Sprinchorn, "Ibsen and the Actors." From *Ibsen and the Theatre: The Dramatist in Production*, edited by Errol Durbach. Published by New York University Press. Copyright © 1980 by Errol Durbach.

Errol Durbach, "'The Land without Paradise.'" From *"Ibsen the Romantic": Analogues of Paradise in the Later Plays*. Published by the University of Georgia Press. Copyright © 1982 by Errol Durbach.

James Walter McFarlane, "Drama and the Person: *An Enemy of the People; The Wild Duck; Rosmersholm*." From *Ibsen & Meaning: Studies, Essays & Prefaces 1953–87*. Copyright © 1989 by James McFarlane.

Inga-Stina Ewbank, "Shakespeare, Ibsen, and Rome: A Study in Cultural Transmission." From *Shakespeare and Cultural Traditions: The Selected Proceedings of the International Shakespeare Association World Congress, Tokyo, 1991*, edited by Tetsuo Kishi, Roger Pringle, and Stanley Wells. Copyright © 1994 by Associated University Presses.

Eric Bentley, "What Ibsen Has Meant." From *Southwest Review* 88, no. 4 (2003): 531–38. Copyright © 2003 by Eric Bentley.

Tanya Thresher, "'*Vinløv i håret*': The Relationship between Women, Language, and Power in Ibsen's *Hedda Gabler*." From *Modern Drama* 51, no. 1 (Spring 2008): 73–83. Copyright © 2008 by *Modern Drama*.

Kristin Brunnemer, "Sexuality in Henrik Ibsen's *A Doll's House*." From *Human Sexuality*, Bloom's Literary Themes, edited by Harold Bloom. Copyright © 2009 Chelsea House Publishers.

Terrance McConnell, "Moral Combat in *An Enemy of the People*: Public Health Versus Private Interests." From *Public Health Ethics* 3, no. 1 (April 2010): 80–86. Copyright © 2010 Terrance McConnell.

Index